What people are saying about …

ASTONISHED

"Mike Erre sets the record straight with a thoroughly biblical and honest look at the unpredictable, untamed, glorious God of Scripture. Read this book, and you'll know your Lord better."

Larry Osborne, author and pastor of North Coast Church

"Astonished pushes us headfirst into the deep end. Reading this book is like drowning—and loving every minute of it. Don't read this book if you want a tame, docile, safe vision of God. Do read this book if you want to be overwhelmed with the glory of who God is."

John Mark Comer, pastor for teaching and vision at Bridgetown: A Jesus Church

"Mike Erre is a young voice worth listening to. He will punch you in the gut while also patting you on the back. Expect to be challenged, inspired, and equipped."

Brad Lomenick, author of *The Catalyst Leader*

"Mike has made a great contribution in *Astonished* by rescuing us from being underwhelmed by the lesser god of our own making and dropping us in the midst of a vision of God that is more and more and more of all that we would ever hope God would be."

Rick McKinley, pastor of Imago Dei Community

"Astonished is a stirring, valuable call for the church to embrace a sense of wonder, awe, and astonishment in its worship of God.

Packed with wise scriptural commentary, engaging personal stories, and the passion you'd expect from a book about God's mind-boggling complexity, *Astonished* is a must-read for anyone who feels stagnant, stuck, or complacent in their faith."

Brett McCracken, author of *Gray Matters* and *Hipster Christianity*

"This book opened my eyes and inspired my heart for God Himself. What more can I say?"

Chip Ingram, author of *True Spirituality* and teaching pastor at Living on the Edge

"If you've grown weary of a tame, domesticated, objectified, overmarketed, American-dream Jesus and instead long to be gripped by the awe and resplendent wonder of the resurrected and exalted Christ, Mike Erre has some thoughts for you to ponder. *Astonished* presents the gospel as it was meant to be."

Barry H. Corey, president of Biola University

"*Astonished* is a deeply moving and provocative look at discovering awe and wonder in the unlikeliest of places."

Steve Carter, teaching pastor at Willow Creek Community Church

"Mike Erre cheers us on to pursue a life of faith, mystery, and wonder in our great Father!"

Dave Gibbons, founder of Newsong and Xealots.org

ASTONISHED

*Recapturing the Wonder, Awe,
and Mystery of Life with God*

MIKE ERRE

David C Cook®
transforming lives together

ASTONISHED
Published by David C Cook
4050 Lee Vance View
Colorado Springs, CO 80918 U.S.A.

David C Cook Distribution Canada
55 Woodslee Avenue, Paris, Ontario, Canada N3L 3E5

David C Cook U.K., Kingsway Communications
Eastbourne, East Sussex BN23 6NT, England

The graphic circle C logo is a registered trademark of David C Cook.

The website addresses recommended throughout this book are offered as a
resource to you. These websites are not intended in any way to be or imply an
endorsement on the part of David C Cook, nor do we vouch for their content.

Unless otherwise noted, all Scripture quotations are taken from THE HOLY
BIBLE, NEW INTERNATIONAL VERSION®, NIV® Copyright © 1973,
1978, 1984, 2011 by Biblica, Inc.® Used by permission. All rights reserved
worldwide. Scripture quotations marked ESV are taken from The Holy Bible,
English Standard Version® (ESV®), copyright © 2001 by Crossway, a publishing
ministry of Good News Publishers. Used by permission. All rights reserved.

LCCN 2014930108
ISBN 978-1-4347-0537-2
eISBN 978-1-4347-0752-9

© 2014 Mike Erre
Published in association with Yates & Yates, www.yates2.com.

The Team: Alex Field, John Blase, Amy Konyndyk,
Nick Lee, Tonya Osterhouse, Karen Athen
Cover Design: Nick Lee
Cover Photo: Shutterstock

Printed in the United States of America
First Edition 2014

1 2 3 4 5 6 7 8 9 10

012714

To our new family at EvFree Fullerton:
As we journey together, may we never lose our sense of
awe and wonder at what God has done for us in Jesus

ACKNOWLEDGMENTS

A big thank-you to:

Curtis Yates—for believing

Don, Alex, John, and the wonderful folks at David C Cook—for their expertise and hard work

The elders, staff, and community at EvFree Fullerton—for daring to dance together

Justina, my sweet love—for your blessing

Nathan, Hannah, and Seth—for the best study breaks ever

To my many mentors in the way of Jesus: I'm inevitably fearful that I haven't fully given credit to the many authors, speakers, pastors, professors, and friends who have shaped my thinking over the years. Where your thinking ends and my thinking begins remains fuzzy. I have long abandoned the idea that I have any original thoughts.

CONTENTS

‖‖‖

THE GOD WHO GETS BIGGER

This is a book about the wildness of God and the adventure of faith.

In C. S. Lewis's *Prince Caspian,* four British schoolchildren find their way into the magical land of Narnia—where animals talk and the land is ruled by the great lion Aslan—and embark on a series of adventures that parallel different aspects of biblical faith. Aslan is the Christ figure in the series, and through him, Lewis makes many insightful points about the nature of God and faith.

One of the most profound moments in *Prince Caspian* occurs when the youngest child, Lucy, sees Aslan after searching for him for a long time:

> "Aslan, Aslan. Dear Aslan," sobbed Lucy. "At last."
>
> The great beast rolled over on his side so that Lucy fell, half sitting and half lying between his front paws. He bent forward and just touched her nose with his tongue. His warm breath came

all round her. She gazed up into the large wise face.

"Welcome, child," he said.

"Aslan," said Lucy, "you're bigger."

"That is because you are older, little one," answered he.

"Not because you are?"

"I am not. But every year you grow, you will find me bigger."[1]

I love that line—"Every year you grow, you will find me bigger." The more Lucy grows, the bigger Aslan gets.

The same thing happens in the New Testament with Jesus. Jesus started out as the son of Mary and Joseph. He learned and grew and was lost at the temple when He was twelve. At thirty He began His public ministry in His hometown, and after His first sermon, the hometown crowd attempted to throw Him off a cliff!

He performed miraculous signs and miracles, and gathered a crowd around Him. He selected twelve to be in His inner circle, though they often were shortsighted, small-minded, and missed the point completely. Even when Peter acknowledged that Jesus was the promised Messiah, Jesus immediately began correcting his misunderstanding of what that meant exactly. It took them a while to fully understand the nature and scope of Jesus's mission.

But the longer they walked with Jesus, the bigger He got. And by the time He rose from the dead, those earliest Christians were forced to rummage through both the Old Testament and the Greek language for concepts and words exalted enough to accurately describe Him.

Jesus is the Word who was God and who was with God in the beginning (John 1:1).

Jesus is the radiance of God's glory and the exact representation of His being (Heb. 1:3).

Jesus is the image of the invisible God (Col. 1:15).

In Jesus, the fullness of deity dwells in bodily form (Col. 2:9).

Jesus is the author and perfector of faith (Heb. 12:2).

John, whose intimacy with Jesus led him to modestly refer to himself as "the one Jesus loved" (John 20:2) saw the risen Christ on the island of Patmos late in his life and fell down, as though dead, at the sight of Him.

The more we grow, the longer we walk with Him, the bigger Jesus should get.

More often than not, however, the opposite seems to be true. Those who follow Him, myself included, are more content to shrink-wrap Him into doctrines, traditions, institutions, and policies, so He becomes smaller and smaller instead of larger and more mysterious. Instead of being astonished by God, we grow easily bored.

And as He becomes smaller, He becomes more easily co-opted; more easily declared to be "the Blessor of my agenda and prefer-ences." That is what makes shrinking Him down so attractive.

The ironic thing is most of the domesticating of Jesus is done in the name of Christianity by the very people who should be protect-ing His holiness and grandeur.

It is this temptation, of course, that has always plagued the people of God. The minute God chose to not use any physical form in reveal-ing Himself to the Israelites, the temptation arose for Israel to define His form for Him. (And that is just what they did with the golden calf.)

But it is Christianity itself, at least as it is classically defined, that has become the form now used to give God structure, shape, and understandability. And this particular form, like all others, simply isn't large enough to contain Him.

This is a book about how Christianity has become a substitute for real, vital, biblical faith.

In the Scriptures, faith is synonymous with confidence, trust, won-overness, and being firmly persuaded. It is far more than mere intellectual agreement with a list of facts. It includes intellectual agreement, of course (and facts!), but is more about how one lives in trusting confidence of those facts rather than checking off doctrinal statements. Faith is, at its core, a relational concept (more about this later). The writer of Hebrews famously defined faith as the "confidence in what we hope for and assurance about what we do not see" (Heb. 11:1).

Notice the connection between faith and "what we do not see." According to the Scriptures, the opposite of faith isn't doubt; it's sight (i.e., trusting in what you can see—2 Cor. 5:7). This distinction becomes crucial for the journey of faith in Christ.

Since God appeared to His people without form, He invited them to trust in what they could not see. But the people preferred to follow and worship something they could see, so they fashioned a golden calf.

The opposite of faith (trusting in what you can't see) is sight (trusting in what you can see). The impulse to domesticate God comes from our discomfort at not being able to see, understand, or perceive God. So we seek to make Him "see-able"—understandable, controllable, predictable.

Of course, we are far more sophisticated in our idolatry than the ancient Israelites—golden calves are only welcome on Wall Street these days. But the temptation for us is no less real. Instead of fashioning physical forms, we fashion intellectual forms—ways in which God must make sense and fit into our doctrinal schemas.

This is a book about the reintroduction of wonder, awe, and mystery into biblical faith.

In our quest to make God and faith understandable, we settle for principles, techniques, and steps. Want to know God's will? Here are four easy steps. Want to know why God permits evil? Here are three great principles that begin with the letter P. There is a place for this, of course, but it feeds the pervasive illusion that God is genuinely interested in making Himself explainable to our finite minds. But much of the biblical record reveals otherwise.

The problem is that all the steps, principles, and techniques become substitutes for faith rather than explanations or applications of it. It is easier to trust in formulas and steps than the unpredictable and untamed God of the Bible. But we can never be astonished by formulas and principles. Steps and techniques cannot sustain the life of faith. Only the God who gets bigger can do that. So let us do the work necessary to be surprised by Him again, to stand amazed at and in awe of His greatness and majesty.

This book is divided into three sections. The first section deals with the nature of God. When we understand a bit more about the kind of God the Scriptures reveal, we shouldn't be surprised by His insistence on faith. The God of the Bible is unpredictable and not always easily recognized. At times, God hides from His people for reasons we'll examine. Sometimes we hide from Him. Perhaps most importantly, God brings us to the end of ourselves so that we actually have to trust Him and nothing else.

God surprises us by revealing Himself in the most unexpected places and in the most unexpected ways. This has to do both with who God is and who we are and why faith describes the arrangement God is most interested in with us.

The second section examines the nature of faith and why faith is difficult for us. Faith demands surrender, which is antithetical to the American values of success and accomplishment. Faith demands we remain comfortable with mystery and tension, which wars against our perpetual need to label, categorize, dissect, and understand. God is simply too big to fit into our classifications. Faith also requires desperation. Jesus isn't for people who have everything figured out or have other options.

The third and final section looks at the nature of the faith-filled life. Faith is a new way of seeing everything. Faith is waking up to God's presence and work all around us. It beckons us out of our comfortable sacred/secular dualisms and into a moment-by-moment awareness that every instant is filled with the promise and opportunity of God's purpose.

Faith is difficult. Living a life of faith even more so. This is a book about why that is. And why, for our sake, it is a good thing.

THE NATURE OF GOD

Chapter 1

_{|||||||||||||||||||||||||||||||||||||||||||||||||||||||||||||||||||||||||||||||||||||||||||||}

DUST AND BONES: THE DIFFICULTY OF HUMAN LIFE

I'm a bit embarrassed to admit that I am a huge fan of infomercials. I have a friend who specializes in producing the half-hour sales pitches that appear on my television in the middle of the night. What is so fascinating to me is how the product in question grows in my heart from "the dumbest thing I've ever seen" to "I need this" in the course of thirty minutes. My friend tells me that what looks like an extended low-budget commercial is actually a well-thought-through and intentionally crafted marketing experience designed to erode every potential objection a buyer may have for not purchasing the product. And it works!

When my wife and I were first married, we were taken in by something called the Ab King. The promise of the commercial was that the Ab King would send gentle currents of electricity through a belt and into my abs, causing them to constrict as if I were doing a sit-up. (If you have ever seen me, you'd understand why such a product was attractive.) Worn long enough, the Ab King promised to turn my stomach from a pony keg into a six-pack.

Once lured in, we were suckers for the promise of all gain and no pain, so we quickly called the 800 number. Two easy payments of $19.99 later, we awaited the brown package at our front door that signified the introduction of my abs to the King. Alas, we were bound for disappointment. Instead of a gentle electrical current, the Ab King delivered a jolt of electricity to my gut that felt as if a red-hot fork were being repeatedly jabbed into it. Needless to say, my abs still need work.

I have resisted the siren call of infomercials ever since, though I do enjoy learning their tricks. I am sure it is more nuanced than this, but advertising seems to work best when it follows a simple formula: create a need and then fill it. Create desire, then offer satisfaction. Sell fear, then offer hope. Even when I know this is what is happening, it still almost works. That is the promise of every new product: that somehow, some way, my life will improve if I buy what they're selling. My life is incomplete, so the story goes, and this will help me look/smell/feel/live better. Gadgets promise to be smaller, faster, lighter, and able to do more. Waiting in line to buy the next big thing is now commonplace.

It's true, of course, that most of what we're sold doesn't live up to its promise. It is the rare product that actually makes a real difference in the lives of consumers. If we're lucky, we enjoy our stuff for a season, then discard it to make room for more. But, inevitably, most of our stuff disappoints, leaving us perpetually in search of the next new thing.

This is the story of the American consumer. This is the free-market, commercialized language and environment we hear and see every day: there is something wrong, something empty in our lives, causing us to feel incomplete and unsatisfied. If we buy or experience product X, we'll never be the same again. We'll find joy and fulfillment, and our ordinary lives will be transformed into something glorious. Rarely are marketers that obvious about it, of course. But that's the basic premise. We are the most commercialized people on the planet, and we'd be fools to think the language and concepts of the free-market economy haven't made their way into our churches and our view of God.[1]

CONSUMING JESUS

How many times has the Christian story been told like this:

> There is a God-shaped hole in your heart, a sense of alienation and incompleteness that you try to fill with sex, drugs, money, success, or whatever. None of those things have worked; they haven't filled the void in your life and only leave you wanting more.
>
> Jesus promises to fill that hole; *He* is the only thing that fits. He'll come into your life and give you meaning, significance, and purpose. You'll feel complete. He's the only one who can satisfy what your soul truly longs for.

There are dozens of variations of this version of the gospel, but they all essentially take the language of the free-market economy and offer Jesus to us instead of product X. Like every other product that promises us fulfillment, Jesus becomes simply another consumer option, offered to us as a way to gain fulfillment and satisfaction, except this time on a cosmic scale.

The problem, obviously, is that this version of the gospel isn't really true. Jesus never made these promises. How many of us still feel incomplete, inadequate, or unfulfilled, even with Jesus? I've learned that Jesus is like the Ab King—full of promise—but He fails to deliver. We get this huge guarantee of how Jesus will complete us, then we find out He's just like every other product we've tried. We may enjoy Him for a season, but sooner or later, He disappoints us, just like everything else.

Unless ...

Unless Jesus isn't a consumer product.

Unless this consumer gospel isn't the real gospel, but only a free-market translation of something that is, in fact, not biblical at all.

Unless Jesus never really promised to remove our dissatisfaction, emptiness, or uncertainty.

Whether or not we know it, most of us relate to God in the same way we relate to the Ab King or any other consumer product. The church is often a willing accomplice in this. There is a void at the core of us that causes us to imagine that there is something somewhere that will fill us and cause us to be whole. That much is true. Whether we call it sin, brokenness, weakness, or simple human limitation matters not. The empty space in all of us is what drives us to turn to something to make life better and make us feel more complete. The church steps into the public square proclaiming the impotence of every other object to fill that space in us apart from God through Jesus.

Certainly there are many ways in which entering into a relationship with God *does* fulfill us; but so often the appeals we make in the name of the gospel use the same logic that drives the sales of the Ab King. Create a need, then show how Jesus (or product X) meets that need.

The problem is that God rarely cooperates with our sales guarantees. There is no place in Scripture where God promises to meet our needs, fill the hole in our hearts, or make our life easier. *In fact, God usually does just the opposite.* That is one reason why so many are disappointed in God. We've made promises for Him that He doesn't make for Himself. Using the language of free-market consumerism to bring people to Christ actually hurts them in the long run for the simple reason that Jesus often introduces difficulty, tension, and uncertainty into our lives. If we've promised people that Jesus will remove the bumps and bruises of life, then they'll be unpleasantly surprised to find He'll frequently introduce bumps and bruises as part of the journey of faith.

And that is the crux of this book: so many of the things we look to God to take away are things He wants to use to draw us deeper into His kingdom.

Mystery.

Paradox.

Tension.

Unfulfilled desires.

Longing.

Emptiness.

Separation.

Loneliness.

Difficulty.

Futility.

Loss.

Grief.

God will use all of these and more to draw us to Him. God isn't the author of all the pain that comes our way, but I do think He values what this kind of pain *does*. Those things listed above effectively put us into the kind of spiritual soil out of which faith, trust, and love grow. God takes us to places where we can't figure it out or depend on our resources or intelligence. He does it because He wants us to trust *Him*, not our formulas, spiritual disciplines, or knowledge of the Bible. He draws us onward, using the acute sense of limitation and sorrow we feel, to bring us to the place where we "don't know" and "can't see" so that we'll reach for Him and grab hold of Him, after there is no other place to turn.

DIFFICULTY AND FRUSTRATION

The opening chapters of Genesis are quite remarkable. We meet God as Creator—a being so powerful He simply spoke the universe into existence. We learn that the universe was the product of intelligence and design, specifically created for human life. We see that human beings stand alone in God's good world as those who are unique bearers of the divine image, created to cogovern as God's representatives over the earth and its inhabitants. Our rulership over the world and everything in it was to be done with God's help, according to His design and for His glory and honor. Human beings were to be signposts and representatives of God's wisdom and creative goodness on the earth.

In Genesis 2, further details emerge about the creation of man and woman. Adam was created first. The man (*adam*) was made to work and care for the garden God called Eden. We are told that he was made from the dust of the ground (the Hebrew word is *adamah*) and was named in relation to it (the *adam* was named after the *adamah*). He was connected to creation because he was both made from it and designed to cultivate and care for it. He was made to find meaning, purpose, and significance in his labor in the garden.

Later in the same chapter, the woman was created out of the side of the man. The man named her, saying, "she shall be called 'woman' [*'ishshah*], for she was taken out of man [*'ish*[" (Gen. 2:23). Like the man, the woman was named in relation to her origin, and this name gives us clues as to where she was to find purpose, meaning, and identity. As we have seen, the man was named in relation to the ground. He came from it and was to work it, finding in his labor purpose, meaning, and significance. The woman was created because no "suitable helper" was found for the man. In English this sounds like the man needed an administrative assistant or something. It is important to note that *helper* (*ezer*) was a word used of God in the Old Testament when He would rescue or help Israel. It was also used to describe the sending and receiving of military aid. A better translation of *ezer* is "ally." The point is that *helper* is a strong word; no trace of inferiority is implied.

Because the woman was created to be a complement and companion to the man, she was made from the man's side. It is significant that she was created from the *side* (not head or feet) of the man. She was to be an equal and a complement. It was in and through her relationship to the *'ish* that the *'ishshah* was to derive meaning, purpose, and significance, in the same manner as the *adam*'s relationship to *adamah*. It is important to understand the relationship between the man and woman and their names in order to fully appreciate what God did to each of them when they rebelled in Genesis 3. God created the man to work and find significance, meaning, and purpose in his labor; and He created the woman to find significance, meaning, and purpose in her relationship to the man. The way they were each named reflected this reality.[2]

As the story continues, our first parents were not content to be made in the image of God; they desired to be like God Himself. That was the essence of the serpent's temptation: that they could be like God, knowing the difference between good and evil. Adam and Eve abandoned their trusting and intimate relationship with God when they disobeyed God's direct command to not eat from the Tree of the Knowledge of Good and Evil. Immediately their eyes were opened, and they hid from each other and from God. God soon discovered their rebellion and, in response, issued judgments against the serpent, the woman, and the man. Note how God spoke to the woman:

> To the woman he [God] said,
>
> > "I will make your pains in childbearing very
> > severe;
> > with painful labor you will give birth to
> > children.
> > Your desire will be for your husband,
> > and he will rule over you." (Gen. 3:16)

Notice the two judgments given to the woman. The first was increased pain in childbirth. While this may strike us as a bit random or arbitrary, this "curse" is related to the command given the woman and the man in Genesis 1:28: "God blessed them and said to them, 'Be fruitful and increase in number; fill the earth and subdue it. Rule over the fish in the sea and the birds in the sky and over every living creature that moves on the ground.'" The first command given to Adam and Eve was to fill the earth and increase in number. The woman was the vessel through which the earth would be filled. Childbearing was central to her purpose and identity. God frustrated her ability to joyfully "fill the earth." Obviously she was still able to give birth, but now there was (more?) pain and sacrifice involved.

Second, God said that her desire would now be for her husband and that he would rule over her. The word *desire* doesn't refer to sexual desire but rather the desire to master or exert control over something. It is the same word used in Genesis 4:7 when God confronted Cain about his anger toward his brother: "If you do what is right, will you not be accepted? But if you do not do what is right, sin is crouching at your door; it desires to have you, but you must rule over it." Here *desire* is used to describe sin's desire to control Cain.

Under the curses of Genesis 3, the woman would "desire" to control the man, and the man would "rule" over her. The word *rule* is the same word used of kings who reign over their subjects. Whereas Genesis 2 ends with the man and woman married, naked, and unashamed, living in complete intimacy and union, their relationship in the Genesis 3 world was now a struggle for power. They blamed each other for their disobedience; they were now in competition with each other for control. This was never God's intention for male/female relationships but is the reality after the fall.

Note again the strategic nature of the judgments. God frustrated the impulse and capacity of the woman to fill the earth in the first judgment. Then the "suitable helper" relationship between the man and woman was frustrated. Again, God created the woman to find meaning, purpose, and significance in both her role as child-bearer and "suitable helper," but God introduced difficulty into both roles. Instead of trusting intimacy, the man and woman would fight each other for control of their relationship. The point is that God frustrated the woman in *exactly the places* he designed the woman to find fulfillment.

Consider the judgment given to the man:

> To Adam he said, "Because you listened to your wife and ate fruit from the tree about which I commanded you, 'You must not eat from it,'

> "Cursed is the ground because of you;
>> through painful toil you will eat food
>>> from it
>> all the days of your life.
> It will produce thorns and thistles for you,
>> and you will eat the plants of the field.
> By the sweat of your brow
>> you will eat your food
> until you return to the ground,
>> since from it you were taken;
> for dust you are
>> and to dust you will return." (Gen. 3:17–19)

Here God frustrated man's relationship to the ground. Adam was created to find meaning, purpose, and fulfillment in his labor; God knew *exactly* where to frustrate the man so he could not find the significance he longed for. Far from being random, the judgments of Genesis 3 are incredibly strategic; God frustrated the very impulses

He gave the man and woman so that life for them in the fallen world would no longer be easy. He introduced difficulty and futility into human life. He thwarted their attempts to find life apart from Him.[3]

Why is it that no matter how much money we have, we always want more?

Why is that our desires—for sex, food, love, or anything else—are insatiable? At best, our enjoyment of what we crave is fleeting; we know we'll be hungry again for more in a short time.

Why is it that our most intense pleasures suffer from the law of diminishing returns so that it takes more and more to experience them less and less?

Why is it that no relationship will be perfect, no job ultimately fulfilling, and no accomplishment permanently satisfying?

The answer is in Genesis 3.

EMPTINESS AND LONGING

In response to the disobedience of our first parents, God frustrated the man and woman precisely in those places He designed them to find meaning, purpose, identity, and significance. Childbearing is painful, relationships are power struggles, and fruitful labor becomes "painful toil." Creation no longer cooperates with the wishes and work of the man and the woman. As we have seen, God was very intentional and deliberate in His judgments. He made life *difficult* for human beings.

This comes as a bit of a surprise to those who are convinced that God's love for us means He would never do anything to make our life harder. But this is precisely what He did. Not just to Adam and Eve but, by extension, to you and me. And the key point, the even more surprising point, is that He did this *as an act of mercy* in order to drive us back to Him. His judgments were calculated to ensure our continued frailty and dependence so that His now-fallen and rebellious creation would be driven back to reliance upon Him. By introducing difficulty into human life, God heightened humanity's sense of vulnerability while at the same time introduced a hunger and thirst for significance and meaning that only He could supply.

Think about it this way. If money really satisfied, how many of us would continue to search for meaning and significance once we had enough? If pleasure or relationships or success or status finally and permanently met our deep needs for identity and purpose, how many of us would ever look to God for help? How many would turn to Jesus if life were perfect? We hunger to be fully alive. This craving for life manifests itself in many ways: the desire to feel loved and happy; the desire to feel significant; the desire to be recognized, appreciated, and valued; and on it goes. God created us with this hunger because He wants to share Himself and His life with us. He wants us to participate, in some infinitesimal way, in His divine nature (2 Pet. 1:4). Our hunger for real life is insatiable.

God is a genius; He realized that the only way to get stiff-necked, rebellious creatures to return to a trusting and obedient relationship with Him was to use their own self-interest against them. We turn to God because we can't make things work on our own. Our resources, ingenuity, and strengths are insufficient to carve out a truly satisfying life on planet Earth. The judgments of Genesis 3 were enough to guarantee that.

God used the futility, limitation, and frustration of human existence to drive us back to Him.

STAY THIRSTY, MY FRIENDS

Life is difficult. We hunger and thirst for that something that we call *really living*. We taste it at times, but most of human life falls short. That is the way God made life in a fallen world. There is a gap between life as it *should* be and life as it *is*. Every now and then, we get a glimpse of what it means to be *fully alive*. But those glimpses are fleeting and unpredictable. If it were possible to get life from our work, achievements, or relationships, we would. But God makes sure that we can't, so we're either forced to keep searching or to turn to Him.

Life in a fallen world is hard. There are many reasons for this. We hurt each other. We hurt ourselves. According to the Bible, we also have a very real adversary who opposes God's purposes in the world. Creation itself groans under the weight of human rebellion. But some of the difficulty of human life comes from God Himself. Out of love, He frustrates us to drive us back to Him.

That is why relating to God as a consumer relates to a product is so misguided. The promise of the Scriptures isn't that God will erase the difficulty and fallenness of human life; rather, it is that He'll use it to draw us to Him over and over and over again. It is a mistake to market God as the answer to our insatiable desires when He was the one who made certain our desires were insatiable in the first place. God is relentless in His pursuit of humanity; He'll use anything and everything to bring us to the place where we'll acknowledge our need for Him.

How then do we live with this sort of God? What should human life look like when, in Solomon's words, all is fleeting and ultimately meaningless "under the sun" (Eccles. 1:1–3)? The world tells us to

handle the difficulty and frustration of human life by escaping—
being "really alive" is found in something outside of our normal
experience. Las Vegas, online porn, a discreet affair, or drugs and
alcohol all offer a way of escaping the confines of ordinary life in the
pursuit of the next great rush.

The church, on the other hand, often teaches us to pretend disappointment doesn't exist. After all, what godly man should admit to
being disappointed in his sex life or career or family? And what godly
woman should ever confess to being disappointed in her marriage, her
work, or her children? It's much safer to simply pretend all is well.

When we discovered that our third child had Down syndrome,
we received emails from people who were upset with us for being
upset with Seth's diagnosis. It would have been much more comfortable for those folks had we just pretended that we were thrilled.
Deep, visceral grief and honest outbursts of emotion aren't often
welcome in our paint-by-numbers, Kinkade Christianity.

Instead of escape or pretense, Jesus calls us to be alive and thirsty,
allowing disappointment to drive us back to Him. He bids us to keep
on asking, seeking, and knocking, all the while feeling the grief and
sorrow of human life acutely. To sell Jesus on the basis of meeting
felt needs is fine so long as we define how exactly He "meets" those
needs. If meeting those needs means the removal of the sin, sorrow,
and disappointment of human life, then we'll be perpetually disappointed. If meeting those needs means that Jesus uses our unfulfilled
desires to keep us dependent and reliant upon Him, then we're getting close to the secret of the full life that Christ offers.

Chapter 2

||||||||||||||||||||||||||||||||||||||||||||||||||||||||||||||||||||||||||||||||||||||||||

THE GOD WHO HIDES

Some years ago I went through a season of life characterized by relentless panic, anxiety, and deep depression. Coming out of surgery on an injured ACL, I started having regular and ongoing panic attacks, accompanied by a complete lack of interest in anything I had previously found interesting or helpful. I battled for years with the roots of this and, to this day, it has not gone away completely. But during those anxious months at the beginning, God seemed to abandon me completely. I didn't sense His presence in my life. Prayers felt like they bounced off the ceiling and went unheard. Worship was joyless and Bible study was drudgery, which only heightened my anxiety and depression. God felt absent.

I stayed in this dry, desert place for many months. And then I came across a very wise mentor who suggested that dry times are a normal part of the Christian life and they were nothing to fear.[1] I have since discovered that many of us struggle with the same core issue. It seems one of the greatest hurdles in our way to growing in Christ is the apparent absence or hiddenness of God from this world and from our lives. This also serves as an obstacle to those outside the faith. "If God would just show Himself to me right now, I would believe," many say.

Surprisingly (to me, at least), the Scriptures don't shy away from these issues or questions. In fact, the Bible seems to indicate that God regularly hides from His people and that there are reasons why He does this. Understanding the God who hides is a crucial part of growing deeper and more mature in Christ.

GOD SHOWS UP?

One thing we can be sure of is that God exists everywhere. Theologians call this God's omnipresence. There isn't one part of the entire universe where God isn't fully present. There is not one square inch of the earth that is not full of God's glory. So we may speak of God's presence in this regard as God's *general* presence. This just means that God exists everywhere.

When we speak of God "showing up" at some event or church service, we are not speaking correctly. Since God is everywhere, He doesn't show up to a place as if He were busy elsewhere but was so impressed by the zeal of the people He had to find out what was going on. Technically, He is not the one who shows up—we are! When missionaries speak of "taking Jesus" to an unreached people group, we must recognize that Jesus was "there" long before we ever showed up. As it has been said, "There are no God-forsaken places, only church-forsaken places."

What we are talking about when we speak of God "showing up" is God *manifesting* His presence. God's *manifest* presence is when humans can see, perceive, experience, or feel God's presence. It is when God's presence is tangible and discernable. Often God's manifest presence was spoken of in the Old Testament as His *Shekinah glory*. This was God's perceptible revelation of His presence in a specific location. God led His people through the wilderness in the form of a pillar of cloud or fire (Exod. 13:20–22); God descended on Mount Sinai in the form of a dense cloud (Exod. 19:9); God's glory filled the tabernacle (Exod. 40:34–38) and the temple (1 Kings 8:10–12). These were all examples of God manifesting His presence in ways that were perceptible to God's people. So when we speak of God "showing up," what we are referring to is the fact that we can feel or sense God's presence.

But this raises interesting questions: If God can manifest His presence to us, why doesn't He do it more often? Why are desert times necessary in our relationship with God when we don't need them in our other relationships? Why does God seem absent when we need Him most? Why does He seem distant sometimes?

The Bible calls this the "hiddenness of God," which raises the following question: Why does God allow us to feel His absence when we know He is not absent (at least in the general sense)? Jesus promised to never leave us or forsake us, so why is it a part of the journey of faith that we go through times when we are not consciously aware of Him? We would think that if the creator of the world invaded our lives, we would at least be aware of it. If God can make burning bushes and part the Red Sea, why doesn't He let us know He's there? How many of our doubts would be answered (or at least lessened) if we felt His presence in our lives? Why, when God can have us feel His presence, do we often feel His absence instead?

WHAT WE ARE NOT ASKING

Questions about the hiddenness of God are not necessarily dealing with the question about whether or not God exists. There are all sorts of good arguments for the existence of God, but those who *already* believe ask this question. Someone may come to faith in Christ and expect they'll feel His presence at all times. But when that doesn't happen, it becomes natural for us to begin to wonder if there is something wrong with *us*.

In one sense, then, God's presence is obvious. There is sufficient evidence for the existence of the Christian God. We need not doubt He is there. Both in the Psalms and in Paul's letters and speeches, the created order is said to witness to the reality of God's power and glory.

Similarly, we are not asking if God has abandoned us (though it may feel that way sometimes). Jesus was quite clear about this when He spoke of never leaving and never abandoning His followers. Once God invades your life, He does not let go. No one can snatch us out of the hands of Jesus.

Nor is our problem the invisibility of God. God is spirit—a person without a body. We can't see God because spirits are invisible. Even human spirits are invisible. Technically, I don't really *see* my wife; I see my wife's *body* (which is good enough for me!). That part of us that thinks, feels, decides, and relates is not visible to our physical senses. So it is with God, except, in His case, He does not have boundaries (in the same way we do). He is infinite.

So when we wrestle with questions about God's hiddenness, we are not asking questions about God's existence, invisibility, or reality in our lives. We may question those things, but I want to focus on the questions asked by those who already believe when they wonder why they don't feel or see God's presence in their lives. Why, if we are God's children, does God feel so distant? We look around at good parents in the world and notice that moms and dads answer their kids when they ask them to do something. They do not remain silent or aloof. They offer tangible evidence of their love and attention. Why doesn't God do the same thing with His children?

THE GOD WHO HIDES

We begin by establishing that God's hiddenness is a normal part of the Christian experience. (To disclaim, again, in one sense God can't hide any more than He could shut off the glory of the heavens or remove His imprint from human beings; but in another sense, God can veil Himself from our conscious awareness.) Several times in the Hebrew scriptures God hides Himself from His people. Isaiah, right in the middle of a section where he was reminding the Israelites how real and huge God is and how empty idols are, paused and reflected and said: "Truly you are a God who has been hiding himself, the God and Savior of Israel" (Isa. 45:15). This is a summary statement of the experience of many in the Old Testament. Certainly, this was not the whole truth of their experience, but it was part of the ongoing nature of their covenant relationship to God. There were times in the midst of affliction that God simply was not manifesting His presence among them. They often did experience His manifest presence, but His felt absence was an ordinary part of their journey as well.

David reflects the reality of the hiddenness of God in the Psalms:

Why, LORD, do you stand far off?
> Why do you hide yourself in times of trouble?
>> (Ps. 10:1)

How long, LORD? Will you forget me forever?
> How long will you hide your face from me?
>> (Ps. 13:1)

Awake, Lord! Why do you sleep?
> Rouse yourself! Do not reject us forever.
Why do you hide your face
> and forget our misery and oppression?
>> (Ps. 44:23–24)

Though God in His being is everywhere, His manifest presence is not. Consider Genesis 3:8:

> Then the man and his wife heard the sound of the LORD God as he was walking in the garden in the cool of the day, and they hid from the LORD God among the trees of the garden.

In this text, the manifest presence of God was limited to certain places in the garden. If Adam and Eve were going to encounter the manifest presence of God, they were going to have to go to a place where there was a visible representation of the presence of God. Even before their sin, it seemed the manifest presence of God was not their ongoing experience. It seems it was something they could draw near or hide from, depending on where they were in the garden.

The theme of God's hiddenness is carried forward into the New Testament. Paul quotes an early Christian creed in his letter to the Philippians:

> In your relationships with one another, have the same mindset as Christ Jesus:
>
> Who, being in very nature God,
>> did not consider equality with God something
>>> to be used to his own advantage;
> rather, he made himself nothing
>> by taking the very nature of a servant,
>> being made in human likeness.
> And being found in appearance as a man,
>> he humbled himself
>> by becoming obedient to death—
>>> even death on a cross! (Phil. 2:4–8)

Several texts in the New Testament teach that God was most fully and finally manifest in the presence of Jesus Christ. The incarnation of God Himself in the bodily form of Jesus was God's clearest revelation of Himself (Col. 1; Heb. 1; John 1). Obviously, God's manifest presence was felt in other ways at other times, but the time when God's presence was manifested more than at any other time was in Jesus of Nazareth. And yet the New Testament describes Jesus as having "made himself nothing" (other translations will use the phrase "emptied himself") (Phil. 2:7). This doesn't mean that Jesus stopped being divine, but that He veiled His divinity … He *hid* it. To some degree, Jesus's divine attributes and divine nature were hidden during His time on earth.

This means there was nothing obvious about Jesus of Nazareth that would have led someone to say, "There is God in human form." As Isaiah wrote about the coming Messiah hundreds of years before the birth of Christ:

> He grew up before him like a tender shoot,
>> and like a root out of dry ground.
> He had no beauty or majesty to attract us to him,
>> nothing in his appearance that we should
>>> desire him.
> He was despised and rejected by mankind,
>> a man of suffering, and familiar with pain.
> Like one from whom people hide their faces
>> he was despised, and we held him in low
>>> esteem. (Isa. 53:2–3)

He veiled His glory and divine attributes. Certainly, at times, He revealed His glory: feeding the 5,000, walking on water, raising the dead, knowing others' thoughts, etc.; but these were exceptions rather than the rule. Often Jesus kept the truth of Himself hidden from those around Him. He would ask those who had seen His miracles not to tell anyone about them; He refused to perform miracles on demand and dismissed Satan's offer to dazzle the crowds. When Peter and the disciples confessed Jesus was the Messiah, His first response was to warn the disciples not to tell anyone who He was. At times, some were even "kept from recognizing" Him (Luke 24:16).

Even the transfiguration, the time when Jesus was literally radiating light and glory in front of two disciples, is evidence of the hiddenness of God. My friend J.P. speculates that nothing special happened to Jesus in that event; but what actually happened is that, just for a moment, Jesus ceased hiding. He allowed the glory that was true of Him at all times to be visible, for a second, to the disciples around Him. Jesus regularly chose to hide His glory. This means, ironically, the time of the greatest manifestation of God was also the time of His greatest hiding.

Who were the first to recognize the birth of Jesus? Shepherds, whose testimony was not counted in a court of law since they were considered ritually unclean and untrustworthy. Angels manifested themselves to shepherds to announce the birth of the Christ—not to kings, priests, or prophets. Jesus was born in Bethlehem, one of the least notable and most unimportant places in Judea. There was no prestige or glory surrounding His birth; it was veiled from the eyes of the rich and the powerful.

So, too, His resurrection. Jesus first revealed Himself to women, whose testimony was not fit for court unless backed up by a husband or male family member. Women were considered unreliable witnesses in the first century, so we see again that at the peak of Jesus's glory through His resurrection, He revealed Himself to people who would most likely not be believed.

It wasn't just Jesus's identity that was hidden. Often the true meanings of His teachings were hidden too. Jesus was asked why He taught in parables in Matthew 13:

He replied, "Because the knowledge of the secrets of the kingdom of heaven has been given to you, but not to them. Whoever has will be given more, and they will have an abundance. Whoever does not have, even what they have will be taken from them. This is why I speak to them in parables:

"Though seeing, they do not see;
    Though hearing, they do not hear or understand.

    In them is fulfilled the prophecy of Isaiah:

"'You will be ever hearing but never
            understanding;
    you will be ever seeing but never perceiving.
For this people's heart has become calloused;
    they hardly hear with their ears,
    and they have closed their eyes.
Otherwise they might see with their eyes,
    hear with their ears,
    understand with their hearts
and turn, and I would heal them.'

But blessed are your eyes because they see, and your ears because they hear. For truly I tell you, many prophets and righteous people longed to see what you see but did not see it, and to hear what you hear but did not hear it. (v. 11–17)

In essence, Jesus replied that He was veiling His teaching from those whose hearts were not open to it. Later in that same chapter, Jesus spoke of His kingdom as being manifested and spread through subtle and hidden ways (like a tiny mustard seed or a bit of yeast hidden in dough). He compared His kingdom to treasure hidden in a field (Matt. 13:44). The primary means by which the kingdom will spread is hidden and undetectable to those who don't see it.

These passages may raise more questions than they answer, but they are sufficient to demonstrate that God's felt absence and veiled presence is nothing out of the ordinary. The Christian life is a life where the manifest presence is enjoyed, experienced, and celebrated, but the manifest absence of God is to be equally experienced and learned from as part of the normal Christian journey. This will be great news for some of us; many of us have gone a long time without sensing God's presence or experiencing dramatic answers to prayer.

WHY GO?

Why does God sometimes withdraw His manifest presence from our conscious awareness? While we can't fully know the mind of God on this, there are clues given throughout the Scriptures.

First, God hides from us so that we can hide from Him (Gen. 3:8). The most dramatic way we hide from God is by sinning. Isaiah 59:2 says, "But your iniquities have separated you from your God; your sins have hidden his face from you, so that he will not hear." Three times in Romans 1, Paul writes that the present form of God's wrath consists in God *giving us over* to our desires and rebellion. In Ephesians 4, Paul exhorts his readers to not grieve the Holy Spirit of

God in us. And in 1 Thessalonians 5, Paul urges his audience to not quench the work of the Holy Spirit. Our sin interrupts and distorts the intimacy God wants with us. God allows us to hide from Him if we want to. If you feel like God is hiding from you, the first question you must ask yourself is whether or not you are hiding from Him. God doesn't hide from us *only* because of our sin, but we must at least be open to the idea that continual rebellion against God prevents us from experiencing the full life Jesus offers. When God seems absent, it may be because the way in which we are living quenches and grieves His spirit, so He does feel far away.

Second, God may hide information from us because the timing is not right for Him to tell us what we want to know. Paul writes about the "mystery" of the gospel, "the mystery that has been kept hidden for ages and generations, but is now disclosed to the Lord's people" (Col. 1:26). The Scriptures teach that before Jesus Christ came to earth, much of what the Messiah would do was hidden from people's understanding. There were many clues, predictions, and prophecies, but it was ultimately a mystery; human beings were not allowed to know much about it ahead of time.

Evidently, God waited until the timing was right in order to send Jesus. Paul says in Galatians, "But when the set time had fully come, God sent his Son, born of a woman, born under the law, to redeem those under the law, that we might receive adoption to sonship" (Gal. 4:4–5). He writes in Romans, "You see, at just the right time, when we were still powerless, Christ died for the ungodly" (Rom. 5:6). Peter echoes these thoughts: "He was chosen before the creation of the world, but was revealed in these last times for your sake" (1 Pet. 1:20).

God did not think that the human race was prepared for what Jesus would say and do until He came. At times, God may seem absent and silent because we are not prepared to receive what He is doing. God will wait until just the right time to let us know what He's up to.

Third, God hides so that we may seek Him. When God announced through Jeremiah to the nation of Israel in exile that He would be silent for seventy years, He then made this promise:

> This is what the LORD says: "When seventy years are completed for Babylon, I will come to you and fulfill my good promise to bring you back to this place. For I know the plans I have for you," declares the LORD, "plans to prosper you and not to harm you, plans to give you hope and a future. Then you will call on me and come and pray to me, and I will listen to you. You will seek me and find me when you seek me with all your heart. I will be found by you," declares the LORD, "and will bring you back from captivity. I will gather you from all the nations and places where I have banished you," declares the LORD, "and will bring you back to the place from which I carried you into exile." (Jer. 29:10–14)

I find it interesting that many of us want to claim the part where God promises our prosperity and security, but we don't claim the promise of God *not speaking* for seventy years first. In this text, these two promises are related. The promise of God's silence and then the

promise of God's blessing are connected to each other. The one pre-
pares for the other. God told Israel that He would be found when
they sought Him with all their heart. Jesus said something about
seeking in Matthew 7:

> "Ask and it will be given to you; seek and you will
> find; knock and the door will be opened to you.
> For everyone who asks receives; the one who seeks
> finds; and to the one who knocks, the door will be
> opened.
>
> Which of you, if your son asks for bread, will
> give him a stone? Or if he asks for a fish, will give
> him a snake? If you, then, though you are evil,
> know how to give good gifts to your children, how
> much more will your Father in heaven give good
> gifts to those who ask him! (Matt. 7:7–11)

You don't have to seek something that is fully present to you. You
can only seek something that is hidden. It is only possible to seek
God because there is a sense in which part of Him is hidden. And
God hides from us to allow us to go through the process—and it is a
very important process—of seeking Him. As Paul writes:

> From one man he made all the nations, that they
> should inhabit the whole earth; and he marked out
> their appointed times in history and the boundar-
> ies of their lands. God did this so that they would
> seek him and perhaps reach out for him and find

him, though he is not far from any one of us. (Acts
17:26–27)

THE DARK NIGHT (OF THE SOUL)

John Coe, another mentor of mine, introduced a concept that has brought much comfort. He explored the crazy thought that the dryness I was feeling was actually a gift from God that He would use to draw me deeper into relationship with Him. Though it sounded cliché at the time, Dr. Coe was right. It was not fun or pleasant, but it was good.

Very simply, he argued that times of dryness and distance (what we are calling God's hiddenness) are ways that God moves us from seeking Him for His gifts and benefits to seeking God simply for Himself. I used to think that the reward for following Jesus was peace, joy, blessing, answered prayer, security, meaning, etc., but have come to realize that the reward for following Jesus is Jesus … and nothing else. Those other things may be included as part of following Him, but they are not the point. I realized that sometimes God hides from us in order to wean us off receiving God the way we want and to begin to receive Him on His own terms.

It could sound elementary, I know. But it was quite profound once he explained it to me. Because I came to Christ with my own self-interest in view (I need forgiveness, healing, purpose, help, etc.), God granted me something the ancients called *consolation*—the felt presence of God that trained me toward those disciplines that will be needed to walk with Christ for a lifetime. Worship is transcendent during consolation; Bible reading and prayer are electric. Obedience is easy during this season. The fundamental aspects of following Christ were reinforced by God's felt presence, and I began (still out of self-interest, since the spiritual "high" was so powerful) to change my patterns of living and thinking. But after a while, my relationship with Jesus had to move from being based solely on self-interest (what I would get out of it) toward having the identity and greatness of Jesus as the foundation. Instead of focusing on me, I needed to begin to focus on *Him*. And though it sounds easy in theory, much work was needed to bring that into reality.

Dr. Coe introduced the idea of the "dark night of the soul," something the ancients called *desolation* (sounds horrible, doesn't it?). The big point is that desolation (the felt absence of God) is as much a gift of God to His people as consolation. The earliest Christian writers reflected that both Scripture and experience testified to the reality that there were times when God was real and present in someone's life—they called that consolation; there were other times as one matured in the faith when God felt absent and distant—they called those times of desolation. They noticed that God would bring His people to times of desolation and distance to grow them in the faith.

Times of spiritual dryness can be gifts from God that draw us deeper into His kingdom so that we quit pursuing Him for His gifts and benefits and pursue Him for His own sake instead. This is a massive shift toward spiritual maturity and is similar to what husbands and wives experience in marriage. Often when a couple is dating seriously, there is a rush of romantic energy and excitement. When you are dating you can hold hands for hours, which feels electric, or you can talk into the late hours of the night. The relationship comes easy at this stage. Every moment, every touch, and every aspect of the relationship is amazing.

But after a couple gets married, they don't stay in the honeymoon phase. Now ten minutes on the phone is plenty, and holding hands no longer produces the same result. We all recognize that no healthy relationship stays in that previous euphoric stage. Why? Because it's easy at that stage to be attracted to the euphoria and not the person (to be in love with being in love, if you will). We don't encourage our children to get married only weeks into a relationship, because they can't really see what is going on. We counsel them to wait and grow beyond that stage, because it can be so blinding. What is used to deepen and mature human love? Most often it is conflict, disappointments, and trials—the mutual struggle together to make the relationship work—where you begin to love and honor the person *as they really are* and not as you want them to be.

You can see this clearly in many of the psalms of David. Psalm 34, for instance, is a psalm of consolation, while Psalm 13 is one of desolation. Some psalms are a bit of both mixed together (e.g., Ps. 28).

God wants to grow us beyond just being interested in Him for His gifts. To do that, He removes His manifest presence from our lives. We begin to wonder if we've done something wrong. But the Bible is clear about this: He would never leave us or forsake us, and there is no condemnation for those in Christ. So God must be doing something else in us. It may be simply that He wants us to love/worship/obey/seek Him for His own sake and not for anything we receive. There is something in the struggle that He values. After all, wasn't the nation of God's choosing born out of struggle: an angel renamed Jacob saying, "Your name will no longer be Jacob, but Israel, because you have struggled with God and with humans and have overcome" (Gen. 32:28). We think the name Israel means "one who has struggled with God." An appropriate name for a people of faith, don't you think?

WHAT NOW?

Dry times are a normal part of the Christian life. We can become addicted to the manifest presence of God, so what do we do when we don't "feel" His presence?

First, ask God to set you free from the guilt and shame from not being the perfect Christian you thought you would be. The grace that saved you is the same grace that leads us in our journey with Christ. By myself, I can't change my heart or my mind, but far too many of us labor under the yoke of trying to shape ourselves to be more like Jesus. Accept that you're not perfect yet. This is a normal part of discipleship. Seek to accept and worship God on His terms.

Second, learn to pray bold prayers. Many of us pray very timid, clichéd prayers that sound more like ordering off a menu than begging God for help. How many of us truly feel the freedom of those who prayed in the Scriptures and spoke honestly and passionately to God about their lives? Prayer is not a time to be good but to be honest, to present your real self, as you really are, to God. We have permission to speak freely before Him and to cry out to Him for answers. Learning to pray the Psalms is a helpful way of learning to speak to God this way.

Third, if you are in a season of not "seeing" God or hearing His voice, spend time around those who do. This sounds easy, but very often I want to do just the opposite. I don't want to be reminded that

He can and does and is speaking, just not to me (at least, that's how it feels). Jesus reveals Himself through His body, and those closest to me regularly surprise me with what God is saying to me through them.

Some of you have been operating under huge guilt, shame, and embarrassment, because you've found yourself in a long season of dryness. My prayer is that you would begin to understand that dryness is a normal, healthy, and needed part of the Christian life. It can be a good gift from a loving Father, though it rarely feels that way.

C. S. Lewis sums up this concept on the lips of a senior demon writing to a junior demon about the ways of the enemy (i.e., God):

> Our cause is never more in danger than when a human, no longer desiring, but still intending, to do our Enemy's will, looks round upon a universe from which every trace of Him seems to have vanished, and asks why he has been forsaken, and still obeys.[2]

Chapter 3

‖‖‖

WHY WE DON'T SEE HIM

As we have seen, there are times and seasons in the journey of faith when God "hides" Himself from His people. This is for our good. But there are other reasons why He *seems* hard to find. Yes, at times, He'll hide Himself from us, but there are other factors in the life of faith we must consider. The Bible is full of examples of God's presence and work going unrecognized by the very people who should have recognized Him. I doubt the chief priests or Pharisees of the first century ever believed that the Messiah of Israel could appear right before their eyes and go unrecognized by them. They would have insisted they were the ones *most* likely to spot Him when He appeared. Some of them did ultimately put their faith in Christ, but the vast majority ironically ended up working against Jesus in the name of God.

The consequences of this were immense. Jesus wept over the city of Jerusalem as He approached it, because they didn't recognize the coming of God's Messiah to them.

As he approached Jerusalem and saw the city, he
wept over it and said, "If you, even you, had only
known on this day what would bring you peace—
but now it is hidden from your eyes. The days will
come upon you when your enemies will build an
embankment against you and encircle you and
hem you in on every side. They will dash you to
the ground, you and the children within your walls.
They will not leave one stone on another, because
you did not recognize the time of God's coming to
you." (Luke 19:41–44)

God was (and is) always showing up when He wasn't
expected—though He should have been—and in a manner that
was surprising. Israel had been waiting for the Messiah for well
over one thousand years. It was understood that the Messiah
would come from the tribe of Judah ("The scepter will not depart
from Judah, nor the ruler's staff from between his feet, until he to
whom it belongs shall come and the obedience of the nations shall
be his" [Gen. 49:10]), the line of David ("When your [David's]
days are over and you rest with your ancestors, I will raise up
your offspring to succeed you, your own flesh and blood, and I
will establish his kingdom" [2 Sam. 7:12]), and be a prophet like
Moses ("The LORD your God will raise up for you a prophet like
me from among you, from your fellow Israelites" [Deut. 18:15]).
The more the Hebrew scriptures unfolded, the more focused and
specific the promises regarding the Messiah became. But I believe
one promise was neglected:

> He grew up before him like a tender shoot,
>> and like a root out of dry ground.
> He had no beauty or majesty to attract us to him,
>> nothing in his appearance that we should
>>> desire him.
> He was despised and rejected by mankind,
>> a man of suffering, and familiar with pain.
> Like one from whom people hide their faces
>> he was despised, and we held him in low
>>> esteem. (Isa. 53:2–3)

I doubt many of the religious leaders in Jesus's day would have questioned their ability to recognize Israel's savior when He appeared to them. Yet, for all the prophecies and hints about what the Messiah would be like, they missed Him. Some even went so far as to accuse Jesus of being in league with the great deceiver, Satan. In one of His dialogues with these opponents, Jesus referred to the ironic nature of their rejection of Him:

> I have testimony weightier than that of John. For the works that the Father has given me to finish—the very works that I am doing—testify that the Father has sent me. And the Father who sent me has himself testified concerning me. You have never heard his voice nor seen his form, nor does his word dwell in you, for you do not believe the one he sent. You study the Scriptures diligently because you think that in them you have eternal life. These are

the very Scriptures that testify about me, yet you
refuse to come to me to have life. (John 5:36–40)

So it is possible for the very people who should be most able
to identify the presence and work of God in the world to overlook
His manifestation among them. Whenever we predetermine how or
where or when He'll reveal Himself, we run the risk of missing Him
altogether. Very rarely does He repeat Himself. That is a warning we
dare not ignore today.

It's not only because God hides Himself that He comes and goes
among us unrecognized. We, too, are part of the reason we don't see
God. The trouble may be with our hearts (do we really want to see
Him?) or it may be with our heads (the Western way of looking at
the world). We must be honest about the life of faith if we are to
seek and find the true life that Jesus offers. This chapter attempts to
examine the question, "Why don't we 'see' God more often?"

WE DON'T WANT TO SEE HIM

You have to want to see Jesus to see Him. As we saw in the last
chapter, God desires us to seek Him. Though He is already present
everywhere, He doesn't reveal Himself where He isn't invited. Mark's
gospel records an instance where Jesus went back to His hometown
and taught in the local synagogue. Many were amazed by His teaching, but there were also some who "took offense at him" (Mark 6:3).
The text says that Jesus "could not do any miracles there, except lay
his hands on a few sick people and heal them. He was amazed at their
lack of faith" (Mark 6:5–6).

He does not force Himself upon us. Jesus is everywhere but must be invited in. Jesus suggests this in Revelation 3:20: "Here I am! I stand at the door and knock. If anyone hears my voice and opens the door, I will come in and eat with that person, and they with me."

Jesus spoke in parables so not everyone would grasp His teaching (Matt. 13:11–15); to really understand Jesus, you had to have "ears to hear." You had to *want* to understand. Jesus kept His teaching on the kingdom partially hidden so that only those who really were hungry for His truth were fed by it. Jesus was perfectly willing to explain the meaning of His parables to those who followed Him (e.g., Matt. 13:11), but they had to work at it. I find it interesting that Jesus didn't always explain Himself to the crowds, often leaving them to puzzle out the meaning of His teaching themselves.

Perhaps the reason Jesus held children up as models of faith (completely contrary to the common views about children of His day) was because they were eager to learn, humble enough to know they needed teaching, and had hearts and minds that were still mold-able enough to be shaped by the upside-down kingdom of Jesus. They hadn't prejudged what God should or shouldn't do, so they were open to His actual work and word among them.

WE DON'T NEED TO SEE HIM

I think most of us would like to see God act in theory, but in prac-tice resist precisely those circumstances that require His action. We'd rather stay in control than truly be in over our heads. We love the illusion of risk but not the reality. So most of our "Christianity" becomes the means by which we attempt to manage and manipulate

God into doing what we'd like. If I give money to God, He blesses me. If I pray for my kids every night, they'll turn out okay. If I stay pure before marriage, I'll have a great sex life afterward. It would be nice if a relationship with Jesus were this clear and easy; the problem is that relating to God in this way doesn't require any *faith*. We think we'll just live by the formulas, and if we keep our end of the contract, God will keep His. This isn't faith; it's risk management.

Our world focuses on assessing and minimizing risk. We want to hedge our finances against future market downturns, and we have home insurance, life insurance, car insurance, fire insurance, flood insurance, and earthquake insurance. Athletes and entertainers can insure parts of their bodies against injury. We sign prenuptial agreements to protect us from the financial ramifications of divorce, and we have health plans to protect us when we are sick. We practice birth control and watch our blood pressure. We wear seat belts and helmets.

We want Jesus to be the same way: all reward, no risk. We don't give ourselves fully to Him, because we are afraid He will send us to China or ask us to become poor or call us to a life of abstinence. We want the illusion of faith as long as we are safe. But walking with God is not a no-risk proposition; it is one of the most dangerous things you can do. Risk is inherent in the life of faith, for risk sets us in places where faith is actually required. Faith and risk cannot be divorced.

We are seldom afraid of opposition that is smaller than us. When we keep our challenges manageable, we not only manage our fear of risk but also squelch our faith. We may look courageous when all we have done is minimize our risk. When God calls us to something, it inspires both faith and fear. It should. God always summons us to something bigger than ourselves. He loves waiting until all other hope has failed and our natural human resources are exhausted. Then He shows up and turns the tide. When He calls us to battle, the opposition will always be greater than the strength we have, because when the odds are in our favor, we may be tempted to give the credit to ourselves. God calls us to live for something higher than our own safety.

Fear tempts us to make safety and self-preservation our highest goals, and the outcome is that we equate the "good" life with risk-aversion. It's not wrong to be healthy and safe, yet so often security and comfort are the values guiding most of our decisions. Fear increases as affluence increases; when we have more to lose, we have more to fear. That is why our worry doesn't decrease as our standard of living increases.

Because we work so hard to stay comfortable and in control, we rarely feel the need for God to come through. Who needs to pray for daily bread when we can simply go buy some? To settle for safety and control, however, is to settle for a life that demands little faith. And little faith demands a little god. We don't see God, because we think we don't need Him.

WE FEAR HE WON'T COME THROUGH

Most of us actively resist circumstances that force us into truly desperate places, places where we have to rely on God *alone*. We do this because we fear disappointment. What if God doesn't come through? What if I pray and God doesn't answer? What if I give but God doesn't provide? What if I risk and end up getting hurt? As we have seen, disappointment with God is a fairly universal sentiment.

60   ASTONISHED

The Psalms are full of complaints against God's absence, silence, and delay. Lament is a consistent theme. But most Christians aren't comfortable with the kind of honesty displayed in the Scriptures. The raw, unvarnished pleas of the psalmists and prophets go against our nice and polite Christian culture. So we work to keep ourselves from having to feel the anguish and sadness that come from being out on a limb and seeing God *not* move the way we need Him to. We manage our risk and minimize our exposure to situations where we are out of control and lack the resources to solve whatever problems we're facing.

Or we can make excuses for God. "It must have been God's will" can either be a profound moment of surrender or a resigned theological cop out. As I sat next to my father's hospital bedside, some well-meaning Christian friends came by and announced that the cancer devouring Dad's insides must have been God's will. On the one hand, I understand what they were saying. God could have healed my dad if He had chosen to do so. But on the other hand, I cannot believe that God *gave* my dad cancer or that God *gave* my son Down syndrome. God's will is expressed in Genesis 1 and 2 and Revelation 21 and 22: tears, sorrow, and death have no place. That is why Jesus told us to pray that God's will be done *on earth as it is in heaven*; why would Jesus have us pray this if what is happening on the earth is God's will?

I don't know why God doesn't answer my prayers the way I want them answered. I wish I could figure Him out. I grieve the evil done to me and by me. I lament the darkness that shrouds our world even on the best of days. The view that all of this is God's will isn't faith; it's a cop out. Jesus clearly revealed a God who has no darkness in Him and who is actively working to renew and restore everything for

His purposes. Faith demands we acknowledge the utter goodness of God, the utter evilness of evil, and the confident hope that God will bring good out of evil. That's it. Far too many of us settle for faith in equations and contracts with God designed to keep us safe and God understandable. Jesus explodes all such formulae and summons us to trust the God we are now to call *Abba*.

WE FEAR HE WILL COME THROUGH

We not only fear God *not* coming through, we also fear Him when He *does* come through. We fear the living God, the God who calls Himself a "consuming fire." At times we'd prefer a God stuck between the pages of the Bible, a book we can open and shut according to our whim. It is the living, breathing Jesus who is so dangerous.[1] We'd rather worship the Bible or worship worship or worship social justice than unleash the consuming fire on today's churchgoing consumers. That's why we schedule our worship services to the second, ensure we have the best audio/visual technology, and produce cutting-edge sermons. Nothing is wrong with these things by themselves, but our insistence on them betrays our confidence in the accoutrements of worship rather than the object of worship. The familiar quote of Annie Dillard says it well:

> On the whole, I do not find Christians, outside the catacombs, sufficiently sensible of the conditions. Does anyone have the foggiest idea what sort of power we so blithely invoke? Or, as I suspect, does no one believe a word of it? The churches are

children playing on the floor with their chemistry sets, mixing up a batch of TNT to kill a Sunday morning. It is madness to wear ladies' straw hats and velvet hats to church; we should all be wearing crash helmets. Ushers should issue life preservers and signal flares; they should lash us to our pews. For the sleeping god may wake someday and take offense, or the waking god may draw us out to where we can never return.[2]

As much as we worry God won't show up, the greater fear is that He will. Who can say what Jesus would do if He walked into our churches? Would He turn over tables and drive people out with a whip (John 2)? Would He rebuke the religious leadership for their hypocrisy and legalism (Matt. 23)? Would He issue praise as well as reprimand for the deeds He sees in the church (Rev. 2—3)? Would someone be struck dead for lying to the Holy Spirit (Acts 5)?

Consider Luke's account of Zechariah's encounter with the angel Gabriel:

In the time of Herod king of Judea there was a priest named Zechariah, who belonged to the priestly division of Abijah; his wife Elizabeth was also a descendant of Aaron. Both of them were righteous in the sight of God, observing all the Lord's commands and decrees blamelessly. But they were childless because Elizabeth was not able to conceive, and they were both very old.

Once when Zechariah's division was on duty and he was serving as priest before God, he was chosen by lot, according to the custom of the priesthood, to go into the temple of the Lord and burn incense. And when the time for the burning of incense came, all the assembled worshipers were praying outside.

Then an angel of the Lord appeared to him, standing at the right side of the altar of incense. When Zechariah saw him, he was startled and was gripped with fear. But the angel said to him: "Do not be afraid, Zechariah; your prayer has been heard. Your wife Elizabeth will bear you a son, and you are to call him John. He will be a joy and delight to you, and many will rejoice because of his birth, for he will be great in the sight of the Lord. He is never to take wine or other fermented drink, and he will be filled with the Holy Spirit even before he is born. He will bring back many of the people of Israel to the Lord their God. And he will go on before the Lord, in the spirit and power of Elijah, to turn the hearts of the parents to their children and the disobedient to the wisdom of the righteous—to make ready a people prepared for the Lord."

Zechariah asked the angel, "How can I be sure of this? I am an old man and my wife is well along in years."

The angel said to him, "I am Gabriel. I stand in the presence of God, and I have been sent to

speak to you and to tell you this good news. And
now you will be silent and not able to speak until
the day this happens, because you did not believe
my words, which will come true at their appointed
time." (Luke 1:5–20)

Years before this event took place, Zechariah and Elizabeth
prayed for a child. As is often the case in the Scriptures, God waited
to answer their prayer until they were well beyond their natural,
childbearing years (why God does this kind of thing so often is
the subject of another chapter). An angel appeared (nearly scaring
Zechariah to death), announcing that God would now answer their
request from all those years ago. Sounds great, right? The appearance
of the angel and the timing of the announcement are so unexpected
that Zechariah can scarcely believe what he is hearing. I don't blame
him. I think I would have reacted the same way. Gabriel, however,
was not pleased and as a sign against Zechariah's doubts, Gabriel
caused him to be mute until the promised child was born. Which
was scarier for Zechariah—God answering His prayer or God not
answering His prayer? Because the presence of God can be so disrup-
tive, we must genuinely consider the possibility that our religiousness
is designed to keep God at arm's length. I'd like to see more of God,
but in small manageable doses, if you please.

WE DON'T REALLY KNOW HIM

Imagine I were trying to describe my mother's voice well enough so
that you could recognize it without having heard it before. I could

talk about the tone of her voice or how she says things; I could describe what she is like or where she comes from. None of that, though, would be much help if you had to pick my mom's voice out from several others. The best way to prepare you to hear her voice would be to allow you to listen to her speak.

The same is true with the voice of God. Information about God or intellectual agreement with some basic facts about Jesus does not substitute for genuine relationship. Recognition comes out of relationship, so one of the reasons we miss seeing God is we don't really know Him. The best way to learn to hear God's voice is to listen to Him speak. One of the significant costs Christians pay for not immersing themselves in the Scriptures is the inability to recognize God's voice, presence, and activity when it occurs outside the pages of the Bible. The Scriptures allow us to learn what God sounds and feels like. Through the Scriptures we learn to recognize how He moves and how He guides and leads His people. So we miss Him when He is moving around us, because we haven't spent enough time learning to recognize His voice.

We must be careful, however, to distinguish genuinely knowing Jesus from merely knowing information about Him. Our churches are full of people who mentally agree with information about Jesus: He was born in Bethlehem; He fed 5,000 people; He died by crucifixion. But Jesus Himself was clear that this kind of knowing isn't the type of knowing He is interested in. In His dialogues with the religious leaders, particularly in the gospel of John, Jesus pointed out that His opponents misunderstood His true identity and purpose precisely because they thought they "knew" God through their traditional theological understandings. Jesus consistently argued that the religious leaders' lack of true "knowledge" of God caused their inability to discern His presence among them. Their faith traditions had been substituted for the real, relational, and experiential knowledge of God He desired.

WE SEPARATE THE SACRED AND THE SECULAR

We come into the world as part of a culture. We are raised, taught, and guided by the background assumptions and principles embedded in the culture in which we live. A crucial part of the journey of faith is to hold these background assumptions up to the truth of Scripture on a regular basis. Because these ideas are so ingrained in us and so much a part of the "normal" way of seeing the world, we may have a difficult time even naming them. Often we may find ourselves interpreting the Scriptures from within our own biased cultural lenses so that Scripture confirms the very lenses we are using to interpret it.

One of the most damaging background assumptions of modern culture to work its way into the church is the distinction between the "sacred" and the "secular." In the "secular" way of looking at the world, God is absent from most (or all, if you are an atheist) of human life and experience. The secular mind-set values what is physical over what is spiritual, what is "here and now" over what is "somewhere else," and what is natural over what is supernatural. Craig Gay comments on the secularization of our worldview:

> [Secularization] is a subtle and largely inadvertent process in which religion—at least as it has

traditionally been understood—forfeits its place in society. Secularization describes a process in which religious ideas, values, and institutions lose their public status and influence and eventually even their plausibility in modern societies.[3]

The secular worldview causes us to live and act as though God does not exist. We may intellectually believe God exists, but He's not *real* to us most of the time. For the vast majority of us, God is mostly absent from our conscious, daily awareness. Sure, we may worship Him or pray to Him, but those are "sacred" times, isolated from our normal everyday life. I go to "church" to worship; I may pray during my "time with God" in the morning; or I go to the homeless shelter to serve. While that is valuable, it leaves the vast majority of our real lives untouched by God's presence, power, and purpose. We live compartmentalized lives—with "sacred" activities and places marked off from the rest of life. God is relegated to certain religious places and times, while I live as a functional atheist the rest of the time.

The cost of this way of looking at the life of faith is high. Following Christ has been reduced to attending weekend services, joining a small group, praying, and reading my Bible, all in a trade-off for the forgiveness of my sins and a ticket to heaven when I die. All of this is essential, but none of it is enough. If Jesus isn't a part of real life, then church attendance and Bible study don't matter. We don't see God at work around us, because we don't even think to look for Him at our jobs, at school, or at home. We walk around on autopilot, not aware of the God at work around us, because we have been conditioned to look and listen for Him only during those "spiritual activities" in our "sacred" spaces.

We are invited to become people who wake up to God's presence all around us, regardless of where we are or what we are doing (more about this later). As we do that, we grow more adept at recognizing the signs that accompany His work and presence (more about that later too). We must intentionally work to overcome the cultural blinders that keep us from looking for God outside religiously sanctioned environments.

WE LOOK FOR HIM ONLY IN THE SENSATIONAL

In our media-saturated culture, only the truly outlandish or sensational makes news. The mundane and ordinary don't sell, so are rarely reported. The same trend is true in our churches. The testimonies that make it in front of our churches are of ex-porn stars and drug addicts coming to Jesus; seldom do we tell or celebrate the story of someone raised in a Christian home who came to Jesus at a young age and has lived a life of quiet obedience since. We hunger for the sensational and the extraordinary. Certainly God does much today that qualifies as truly supernatural and miraculous. But our infatuation with the spectacular can blind us to the ways in which God moves in and through the ordinary and the common.

We don't want boring sermons and church services; we want to be *moved*. We don't want to sing regular worship songs; we want to *feel* the presence of God in our singing. It's not enough to volunteer at church; we want to *change the world*. And in some respects, this hunger for the transcendent is a good thing. But there is a downside. If we think to look for God *only* in the dramatic and sensational, then we won't think to look for Him anywhere else. And if you're like me, most of life is most assuredly *not* dramatic or sensational. If we are only on the lookout for the next spiritual high, then when nothing special happens or we don't get incredibly emotional from a spiritual experience, we assume God never showed up. Yes, at times God will reveal Himself in the spiritually intense moments we crave. But He also brushes right by us in the ordinary, average, and mundane parts of our daily lives. But in our quest for only the spectacular, we won't recognize Him when He meets us and calls out to us the rest of the time.

So the difficulties surrounding the life of faith are not just with God but also with us. While we must recognize the reasons why God might be hiding Himself from us for a season, we must also allow for the reality that we contribute to our own blindness.

Chapter 4

||||||||||||||||||||||||||||||||||||||||||||||||||||||||||||||||||||||||||||||||||||

THE UNPREDICTABLE GOD

I am one of those people who likes routine. I eat at the same places every day, usually ordering the same thing every time. I have no problem wearing the same two or three shirts all week, every week. I like going to bed at the same time each night and getting up at the same time every morning. I drive the same way to work and the same way home at night. I like to go to the same places on vacation. Sounds boring, I know.

I like it this way, because routines allow me to think and dream and create without having to focus on the little things. Routine makes me comfortable. I like things predictable and regular.

This desire for normalcy and predictability isn't a bad thing; it just makes following the God of the Scriptures more difficult. I know that God is a God of order and design and that He holds the universe together with remarkable consistency and intelligence. It's just that I can't quite pin Him down or box Him in. I keep trying to get Him to stay put, but He keeps one step ahead of me, always just out of reach. He continuously disrupts my life and routines, reminding me of how big and majestic He really is. He resists my attempts to confine Him and laughs off my complaints about His unpredictability.

He knows that sometimes I think that if I were running the universe, I would do a better job of managing things. I'd certainly never say it that way or admit it out loud. But every now and again I find myself imagining what it would be like if I were in charge.

I'd cut down on evil, hand out more blessings, and generally be less restrained in the way I'd manage things. I'd show off a bit more; maybe publically smite some folks who needed it, just to remind everyone that I was still around. If I were God, I'd delegate a little less, thank you very much.

On the whole, life with God would just be so much easier if He were predictable. Understandable. Operating according to Generally Accepted Divine Accounting Principles. I'd like Him much better that way. As it is, I can't figure Him out. Grace and love do not lend themselves to easy quantification and calculus. Justice and wrath offend my sense of balance and proportion. He defies my attempts at negotiation. He never moves in a straight line. He dances at the edge of my vision, but when I turn to look at Him, He's already somewhere else.

If I were God, I would be a lot more cooperative.

But as it is, we're stuck with an unpredictable, uncooperative, and completely outside-the-box sort of God. Which makes it difficult when so much of Christianity is for people like me, designed to make Him make sense and to fit into our boxes.

PREDICTABLY UNPREDICTABLE

Part of our problem is that we confuse God's reliability with God's predictability. God is perfectly reliable. His character never changes. He is the same yesterday, today, and forever. His word never fails. He is love. God does not lie, and there is no hint of darkness in Him.

But reliability does not equal predictability. To say that God is always good, faithful, or loving doesn't mean God always makes sense ahead of time. If we learn anything from the portraits of Jesus in the Gospels, we learn that He is unpredictable, and He taught, loved, and lived in ways that were completely unexpected. He was often found where you would least expect the Messiah to be. In so many ways, Jesus turned people's expectations upside down.

Who could have imagined the Creator of the universe invading the earth not in glory, but born to an unwed teenage mother who then placed Him in a feeding trough?

Who could have imagined that when Israel's Messiah appeared, He would be found among the prostitutes, tax collectors, and sinners of His day, gaining a reputation as a glutton and a drunkard (Matt. 11:19)?

Who could have imagined that God would defeat death by dying? Or conquer evil by allowing its triumph on the cross? Or free humanity by bearing upon Himself the cost of human sin and evil?

In Jesus's world, there was a profound belief among the people that the kingdom of heaven was about to appear at any moment. But they were convinced it would appear the way it always had— through God's blessing of His people's military efforts to defeat the pagan cultures around them. And at no festival during the calendar

year was that thought more central than around Passover—the celebration of the deliverance of the Jews from Egypt. So when Jesus
"triumphantly" entered Jerusalem the Sunday before Passover, the
natural reaction of the crowd was to shout "Hosanna" and wave palm
branches—symbols of revolution and revolt from generations earlier.
They were looking for a political savior, a power figure, someone who
would defeat Rome and restore Israel.

Jesus had not come to kill, however, but to die. Military power
could not bring about the kingdom Jesus came to inaugurate. He
wept over the city and died at their hands, forgiving them as they
crucified Him. They were ready to crown Jesus Messiah, but He was
not what they'd expected.

The mystery surrounding Jesus continued after His resurrection.
If I had just risen from the dead, I would be proudly walking down
the streets of Jerusalem during the busiest times of the day, showing
off my scars and gloating a bit over my enemies (and maybe do a
little smiting too). What did Jesus do? He cooked breakfast for His
followers. One of His closest friends thought He was a gardener. He
was consistently not recognized. He just appeared, told people to be
at peace, and then went on His way.

"US" JUST GOT BIGGER

God works to constantly expand our understanding of what it means
to follow Him and understand what His work looks like. His movement takes all sorts of shapes and forms. Once you think you get it
nailed down, He moves in a new way. Religion gives us forms and
shapes for God to fit into, but He constantly proves to be bigger,

wider, and deeper than our boxes. Just when we think we've figured out where God is going next, the wind blows somewhere else. I want to be a person who celebrates the movement of God wherever I find it, but my desire for predictability gets in the way.

It's nice to know Jesus's original disciples had the same problem. In Luke's account, the disciples had just finished arguing about who among them would be the greatest when this little conversation took place:

> "Master," said John, "we saw someone driving out demons in your name and we tried to stop him, because he is not one of us."
>
> "Do not stop him," Jesus said, "for whoever is not against you is for you." (Luke 9:49–50)

I think we can all agree that the fewer demons the better, right? Well, the disciples came across someone casting out demons *and they tried to stop him*. Why? Because he wasn't one of the "official" group of disciples. So they tried to stop the guy who was setting other people free. This wasn't fitting into their "box" of what the work of God should look like (and who should get to do it), so they tried to put an end to it.

I love Jesus's response. He wasn't threatened or jealous. He reminded them that God's "team" is a bit bigger than they thought. God's work simply won't fit into their preconceived categories.

There is an Old Testament parallel to this story in Numbers 11.[1] Moses was complaining to God about the heavy burden of leadership over the nation of Israel. God commanded that seventy trusted elders join Moses in front of the tent of meeting (the place where God spoke to His people in the wilderness).

So Moses went out and told the people what the
LORD had said. He brought together seventy of
their elders and had them stand around the tent.
Then the LORD came down in the cloud and spoke
with him, and he took some of the power of the
Spirit that was on him and put it on the seventy
elders. When the Spirit rested on them, they
prophesied—but did not do so again.

However, two men, whose names were Eldad and
Medad, had remained in the camp. They were listed
among the elders, but did not go out to the tent. Yet
the Spirit also rested on them, and they prophesied in
the camp. A young man ran and told Moses, "Eldad
and Medad are prophesying in the camp."

Joshua son of Nun, who had been Moses' aide
since youth, spoke up and said, "Moses, my lord,
stop them!"

But Moses replied, "Are you jealous for my sake?
I wish that all the LORD's people were prophets and
that the LORD would put his Spirit on them!" Then
Moses and the elders of Israel returned to the camp.
(Num. 11:24–30)

Two men stayed behind and were not an "official" part of the
group that went to the Tent of Meeting. When God's Spirit moved
in them, Joshua had the same reaction as the disciples—they needed
to be stopped. Moses's response was similar to Jesus's. He wasn't
troubled or jealous, but instead wished everyone were like these two.

Like the disciples, Joshua had an idea of how God should work but was then confronted with a God who works differently.

Joshua and the disciples were threated when God moved outside the lines. For Jesus and Moses, God could move however and wherever He wanted. They celebrated the movement of God whenever they saw it. Joshua and the disciples were interested in boundaries—God's work had to fit inside a certain box for it to be "official." Jesus and Moses were more interested in expanding whatever boxes they had.

Joshua and the disciples wanted to restrict who got to participate in God's work—only officially "sanctioned" people were welcome. They focused on "us" versus "them." Jesus and Moses were much more interested in pointing out that "us" was much bigger than they thought. Joshua and the disciples believed that God should move only at certain places or through certain people. Jesus and Moses longed to see others included as the work of God expanded.

I am sympathetic to Joshua and the disciples. I think it would be a lot less confusing if God only moved through officially designated people, places, or activities. As it is, He's tough to keep up with. I never know what He'll do next. As a full-time paid religious person, I understand the desire to restrict God's work to only those who are formally recognized by our religious institutions. But He's too unpredictable for that.

EXPECTING THE UNEXPECTED

The goal, then, is to become the kind of people who recognize and celebrate God's work however and wherever we see it. It's far too easy to be threatened by what God is doing in another community. As sad as it is to admit, there can be a certain sense of competition between churches and spiritual communities. Such jealousy runs counter to God's purposes in the world.

In describing what spiritual birth looks like, Jesus likened the movement of God's Spirit to the movement of the wind (the same Greek word is used for both *spirit* and *wind*). He said, "The wind blows wherever it pleases. You hear its sound, but you cannot tell where it comes from or where it is going" (John 3:8). To embrace the full life of Jesus and His purposes for the world, we must be prepared to see God move and work in all kinds of fresh and creative ways. If God wants all people to be "saved and to come to a knowledge of the truth" (1 Tim. 2:4), then we should not be surprised when we see Him tugging at people in crazy ways. The wind blows where it wants.

We must be very careful to never forget that God is bigger than our boxes. When we confine God to a box, whether it is theological, methodological, or denominational, we run the risk of working against God at the same time we think we are working for Him. *Of course* we do the hard work of discernment and holding everything up to the truth of Scripture. We must be careful about what we affirm as truly "of Christ." I just wish to point out the "of Christ" part is going to be radically bigger, wider, and deeper than what we'd naturally like. Jesus will force us to continually re-examine our boxes in light of His work outside them lest we spend more time defending our boundaries than expanding them. Boxes are fixed in size and shape but don't do a great job predicting or containing the movement of the wind. (Watch your local weather reports for proof!) Both the disciples and Joshua were trying to *stop* what God was doing *in His name*! Unless our view of Jesus keeps getting bigger, we run the risk of quenching God's Spirit in the name of the Jesus we are supposedly following.

So we must be prepared to be surprised by His movement. In the Gospels, Jesus was often found where you'd least expect the Messiah to be. The same thing is true today. Expect to find Jesus where you'd *least* expect Him—more in failure than in success; more in poverty than in luxury; more among the downcast and dubious than the bright and beautiful. If it's really Jesus, we shouldn't be surprised to find Him hidden. He wasn't always immediately recognizable to His first followers; why should we think He'd be any different with us?[2]

The problem is, of course, that the unexpected, unpredictable, and surprising are precisely what we *don't* expect as far as most of God's people are concerned. I am not sure how we would react if Jesus actually revealed His presence at our church services. I doubt He would keep to the order of worship or to our predetermined set lists. None of us are surprised that nothing surprising happens in most of our church gatherings. So we fill the void with *awesome* sermons, *incredible* worship, and *life-altering* programs. Our use of superlatives only underlines our tragic neglect of the unpredictable and surprising God. He rarely surprises us because we haven't invited Him to. We make no room for the unexpected and work hard to control the flow and direction of the service. This isn't all bad, but it does cast doubt on the sincerity of our worship and pursuit of God. Most of us aren't looking for God in the middle of church, because we're far more interested in whether we like the worship or the teaching. I've personally found God to be present more often when I *like* the music and teacher (please note the sarcasm).

The surprising Jesus loves us, yes, but does His best work outside the American church these days. Visit a gathering of Christians in any third-world country, and you'll see what I mean. No chairs, no child care, no canned talk with borrowed illustrations and PowerPoints; just the presence of God among His people. That's the surprise. Jesus is never where you'd expect Him to be. The surest place to find Him is among the sorrowful and suffering. He was found among the lepers, demoniacs, cripples, and the poor in spirit in the first century; He'll be found among the addicts, the diseased, and the down-and-out today. If we want to find Jesus today, we need not look any further than where He told His disciples to look:

> Then the King will say to those on his right, "Come, you who are blessed by my Father; take your inheritance, the kingdom prepared for you since the creation of the world. For I was hungry and you gave me something to eat, I was thirsty and you gave me something to drink, I was a stranger and you invited me in, I needed clothes and you clothed me, I was sick and you looked after me, I was in prison and you came to visit me."
>
> Then the righteous will answer him, "Lord, when did we see you hungry and feed you, or thirsty and give you something to drink? When did we see you a stranger and invite you in, or needing clothes and clothe you? When did we see you sick or in prison and go to visit you?"

> The King will reply, "Truly I tell you, whatever
> you did for one of the least of these brothers and
> sisters of mine, you did for me." (Matt. 25:34–40)

The guides to His kingdom are no less surprising than He is. The poor, the suffering, and the disabled are those who best point the way to Jesus and identify His presence in the world.

I am writing this the week after Christmas. Our church put a ton of time and expense into presenting four Christmas Eve services to the community, full of carols, hymns, and a rousing rendering of the "Hallelujah" chorus! It was amazing.

The week prior to Christmas Eve, our disabilities ministry performed their annual Christmas play. Thirty or so adults and kids with varying disabilities—autism, Down syndrome, cerebral palsy, etc.—acted out the angel's announcement to the shepherds about the coming Messiah. There was dancing and laughing, drooling and prompting, and after ninety minutes of watching, those in attendance could do nothing but stand and applaud at the faces of radiant smiles from the performers.

I couldn't help but compare the two services. I am incredibly proud of our church for offering both. I'm compelled to ask, though, which one better reflects the heart of Jesus? The one filled with tradition, good tidings, and familiar songs? Or the one that encouraged my then three-year-old son to come up on stage and continually interrupt the proceedings?

In learning to recognize the presence of the unpredictable God, we have a sure guide in the person, words, and work of Jesus of Nazareth. Jesus is the best and clearest revelation of what God is really like. Because of this, we know that Jesus will be found among the poor and marginalized; among the outcasts and misfits; and among the meek and the mourning. He spent most of His life in obscurity and, even after His public ministry began, He often warned people to not tell others who He was or what He had done. He was far more interested in proclaiming and embodying the good news about His kingdom to the common people than He was in receiving the validation of the religious establishment.

As best we can, we must cultivate a posture of openness and expectancy when we seek to recognize His presence and work. He'll not always be found in the obvious and the religious or among the grand and mighty people of our age. He is routinely surprising, which is tough for people like me. But following Jesus demands no less. And if it's really Him, if Jesus is genuinely present, then God's people should be prepared to celebrate the creative and ingenious ways that God will show His love to people. We should routinely be surprised, since He is reliably unpredictable.

Chapter 5

THE GOD AT THE END OF OUR ROPE

One of my favorite *Seinfeld* episodes is where George (the lovable middle-ager who has nothing going for him and still lives with his parents) realizes that his life would be far better if he just did the opposite of what he would normally do in every situation. George's friend Jerry convinces him that every instinct he has naturally is wrong, so he should do the opposite. As the episode progresses, and as George takes Jerry's advice, he lands a new job, a new girl, and an apartment of his own.

Following Jesus turns out to be just like that—doing the opposite of what usually comes naturally to us. It is natural to hold a grudge; Jesus calls us to forgive. It is natural to love only those who love us; Jesus calls us to love our enemies. It is natural to look out for our own interests; Jesus calls us to love our neighbors as ourselves.

In His kingdom, the last is first and the first is last. Up is down. Greatness is service. Losing your life means saving it, and trying to save it means you'll lose it in the process. Under God's rule, you can be blessed if you mourn or if you are poor in spirit, and you can be cursed if you are rich and well fed.

It is as if every single human value, priority, or accomplishment falls at the *bottom* of God's value system and those things that human beings naturally despise and reject are highly prized in God's sight.

So I propose a George Costanza form of Jesus followership: we should almost always do the opposite of what comes naturally and easily to us. And that is the answer to the perpetual WWJD (What Would Jesus Do?) question: He would do the exact opposite of what you and I would naturally do in any situation.

The upside-down values of the kingdom of God force us to rethink almost everything. Take, for instance, our understanding of strength and weakness. What is considered strength in American culture is frequently seen in the Scriptures as weakness; and what is seen as weakness by our world is seen as strength in God's eyes.

In the Bible, weakness often looks like strength, and strength often looks like weakness.

Consider the arrest and trial of Jesus. A mob showed up, sent by the religious leadership, brandishing clubs and swords. Peter grabbed a sword and struck a servant of the high priest, severing his ear. We can imagine Peter thinking, *Jesus didn't seem to be* doing *anything; He is* letting *this happen.* Wasn't Peter the one who rebuked Jesus for announcing He was going to be crucified? And here it was. So Peter took matters into his own hands.

It's understandable, isn't it? Swords come in handy when you're scared and everything you believe in is crumbling around you. It's the most natural thing in the world to strike out when you feel threatened.

So Peter's sword, and the impulse to draw it, looked strong but were actually weak. Jesus's restraint, on the other hand, looked weak but was actually the greatest show of strength imaginable. Jesus healed the servant's ear and rebuked Peter, reminding him that He had legions of angels at His disposal. He only had to give the word, and seventy-two-thousand angels would fight to prevent His arrest. Jesus's restraint is the only real strength in the story. The religious leaders, the mob, Judas the betrayer, and Peter and his sword—all are seen as weak when compared to the strength of Jesus.

Jesus was brought before Pilate, the Roman official governing the area of Judea. At one point, when Pilate was confronted by some of the Jewish leadership and their demand to have Jesus crucified, he asked Jesus where He came from. Jesus refused to answer, prompting Pilate to remind Him, "Don't you realize I have power either to free you or to crucify you?" (John 19:10).

I love Jesus's answer. He said, "You would have no power over me if it were not given to you from above" (John 19:11). In other words, Jesus was saying, "Pilate, you don't know what real power is. Yours is derivative. Mine is not."

Pilate was convinced in the strength of his position and authority. And by every human measure, Pilate was strong. And Jesus looked weak: mocked, ridiculed, threatened, alone ... But remember, there is a weakness that masquerades as strength and a strength that appears like weakness. We see both here. Jesus looked weak but was strong; Pilate looked strong but was weak.

The same is true today, of course. How many of us love to get even, have the last word, or punish someone for some real or imagined slight? How many of us pull out our verbal sword when we are angry, cutting and slicing one another with the same violence that Peter used against the servant of the high priest? It feels good to do something, to fight back, to revel in our strength to get our way. It is easy to resort to the strength and power that come from position and authority.

Pilate said, "Don't you realize I have power either to free you or to crucify you?"

We say, "Don't you realize I have the power to hire you?"

We say, "Don't you know who I am?"

We say, "Don't you know what I can do for you?"

And to Pilate, and all of those like him, Jesus says, "What little strength you have was given to you."

Jesus understands the way power works. He knows what true strength is rooted in. Peter and Pilate appeared strong but were weak. Jesus appeared weak but is strong. In Jesus's kingdom, everything is upside down. Strength and weakness aren't what they first appear to be. The crowd with its clubs and swords, the violence of Peter, the betrayal of Judas, the position of Pilate—all of these appeared strong but were not. The willingness of Jesus to be arrested, His forgiveness of those crucifying Him, the glimpses we get of His divine restraint in His conversation with Pilate—all of this appears weak but instead represented the most profound strength conceivable.

THE STRENGTH OF WEAKNESS

The apostle Paul taught this truth in a powerful way. Though he is a big deal to us, Paul was hardly the towering figure he is today to his contemporaries. Through revealing glimpses in his writings, it appears that some in the churches he planted were not that impressed with him. The church in Corinth, particularly, saw him as a bit underwhelming in person. Many were taken by the so-called superapostles—those who, through their sophistry and rhetoric, were much more impressive and dynamic. Paul, many times throughout his two letters to them, defended himself and his apostolic credentials. What is fascinating is how he went about his defense:

> Whatever anyone else dares to boast about—I am speaking as a fool—I also dare to boast about. Are they Hebrews? So am I. Are they Israelites? So am I. Are they Abraham's descendants? So am I. Are they servants of Christ? (I am out of my mind to talk like this.) I am more. I have worked much harder, been in prison more frequently, been flogged more severely, and been exposed to death again and again. Five times I received from the Jews the forty lashes minus one. Three times I was beaten with rods, once I was pelted with stones, three times I was shipwrecked, I spent a night and a day in the open sea, I have been constantly on the move. I have been in danger from rivers, in danger from bandits, in danger from my fellow Jews, in danger from Gentiles; in danger in the city, in danger in the country, in danger at sea; and in danger from false believers. I have labored and toiled and have often gone without sleep; I have known hunger and thirst and have often gone without food; I have been cold

and naked. Besides everything else, I face daily the pressure of my concern for all the churches. Who is weak, and I do not feel weak? Who is led into sin, and I do not inwardly burn?

If I must boast, I will boast of the things that show my weakness. (2 Cor. 11:21–30)

It's like Paul was saying, "Fine. If you want to compare me to these other apostles, let me ask you this: Have they suffered for Jesus like I have? Have they been in danger like I have? Have they been persecuted like I have? Have they been as weak as I have been?"

No pastor today would lead with this list as "proof" of God's call on their life! No bestselling author would have a bio that sounded like this. No, we, like the ancients, are much more impressed with numbers, accomplishments, and titles. But Paul, like Jesus, saw through them to the real source of strength and authority. Paul continued, speaking of visions and revelations he had received from God:

Therefore, in order to keep me from becoming conceited [because of these surpassingly great revelations], I was given a thorn in my flesh, a messenger of Satan, to torment me. Three times I pleaded with the Lord to take it away from me. But he said to me, "My grace is sufficient for you, for my power is made perfect in weakness." Therefore I will boast all the more gladly about my weaknesses, so that Christ's power may rest on me. That is why, for Christ's sake, I delight in weaknesses, in insults, in

hardships, in persecutions, in difficulties. For when
I am weak, then I am strong. (2 Cor. 12:7–10)

We are not sure what exactly the "thorn" consisted of. Some speculate it was a physical malady; others, the emotional and spiritual pressure Paul felt for his churches. Whatever it was, Paul wanted it gone. But God refused. The standard translation of what God said to Paul in response is, "My grace is sufficient for you, for my power is made perfect in weakness" (2 Cor. 12:9). But I think there is a better way to translate this sentence.

A bit of Greek will help us here. Marva Dawn, in her powerful little book, *Powers, Weakness and the Tabernacling of God*, makes (to me) a convincing argument that the standard translation should be reconsidered (I rely on her work for most of this section). A summary of her argument consists of the fact that there is no possessive pronoun to make *strength* God's strength. The Greek could be referring either to Paul's strength or to God's strength. It is ambiguous. Secondly, she argues that the verb translated "made perfect" is better rendered "bring to an end," which is in agreement with its use throughout the rest of the New Testament.[1]

If Dawn is correct, and the verb should be translated "brings to an end," then the rest of the verse cannot be referring to God's power, since God's power is never brought to an end. Instead, the verse makes more sense if it is seen in reference to *Paul's* power; that is, 2 Corinthians 12:9 should be translated instead, "My [God's] grace is sufficient for you [Paul], for your [Paul's] power is brought to its end in weakness."

This is the reason Paul glories in his weakness, for when his power is brought to its end, Christ's power rests on him. In other words, our power must be limited so that God's might be better put on display. Paul's power is brought to its end in weakness; consequently Paul exalts his weakness because through its existence Christ is able to reveal His presence in him. Dawn comments, "Even as Christ accomplished atonement for us by suffering and death, so the Lord accomplishes witness to the world through our weakness. In fact, God has more need of our weakness than of our strength."[2]

The Christians at Corinth had dismissed Paul because he did not demonstrate the credentials of a superapostle. Many back then believed Christian leaders must be charismatic, powerful, and have great and attractive personalities (I'm so glad it's different now, right?). The prevailing cultural model for them was built around rank, status, and achievement. That is the language of "boasting" that Paul used in this letter. It was right and proper for people to boast and demonstrate their status to others. Paul moved in entirely the opposite direction. He listed his weaknesses, persecutions, and sufferings, and then revealed why this was so. God does His best work, Paul said, when we are at the end of our rope.

AT THE END OF OUR ROPE

God's working not through human power but through human weakness is a central theme of the Bible. God used Abraham's age and Sarah's barrenness to give birth to the beginning of the great nation Abraham was promised. Moses wasn't very eloquent and was filled with excuses when God called him to deliver the nation of Israel out of slavery. David was just a kid when he faced Goliath. Peter became the leader of the church only after he denied Jesus three times.

Throughout the Scriptures, this was God's way. He made people strong out of their weakness. He brought them to a place of weakness so He could use them for His glory. He actively limited their power so that His might be put on display. It is not that God comes and makes us strong and then uses us; rather, it is that God brings us to the end of our strength, our wisdom, our trust in self so that we actually have to trust *Him* and not something (or someone) else. This is the paradox of strength and weakness: that I am strongest when I am weakest; I am most usable when I am in over my head; Jesus is most present when I am at the end of my rope.

God's way is not about triumphalism or becoming bigger than life. It is not about reaching a place where all weakness is gone. Instead it is about having my own power limited so that I can discover how God uses my weakness. If you are like me, we resist limitations. I want to make things happen, plow through problems; I was conditioned to overcome obstacles, not recognize weakness and admit it.

But Paul said that the goal is for our power to come to an end. How can I experience God's power unless my own power is limited?

This radically redefines who is considered "worthy" to be used by God. In the middle of a baptism service a couple of years ago, a mother of two teenage sons approached me and said her two boys wanted to be baptized. We talked a bit, and I eventually asked her if she wanted to baptize them herself. In response her countenance changed and she backed away, telling me she was not worthy to do so. I disagreed with her, but she was adamant. I baptized her sons but not without some sadness. If time weren't an issue, I wish I could have asked her some questions:

Are you a murderer of Christians? Because that was what the apostle Paul did prior to becoming a follower of Jesus.

Are you a prostitute? Because that was what Rahab was before she was listed in the great hall of faith in Hebrews 11.

Are you a liar and a cheat? Because that was what Jacob was before he was renamed Israel and gave birth to a nation.

Are you a coward? Because that was what Abraham was when he sold his wife to Pharaoh's harem (twice!) to protect his own skin.

Are you an adulterer or drunk? Because that was what David was when he was king over Israel, writing what would be the worship manual of ancient Israel and the early church.

Have you denied Christ? Publically? Multiple times? Because that was what Peter did before becoming one of the leaders of the early church.

Many more examples could be given, but you get the point. There is no one *worthy* in God's sight. That is what I wish I would have shared with that mother. In fact, God seems to delight in taking the weakest among us and using them to show His power and greatness.

Paul said as much in his first letter to the church in Corinth:

> Brothers and sisters, think of what you were when you were called. Not many of you were wise by human standards; not many were influential; not many were of noble birth. But God chose the foolish things of the world to shame the wise; God chose the weak things of the world to shame the strong. God chose the lowly things of this world and the despised things—and the things that are

> not—to nullify the things that are, so that no one
> may boast before him. It is because of him that you
> are in Christ Jesus, who has become for us wisdom
> from God—that is, our righteousness, holiness and
> redemption. Therefore, as it is written: "Let the one
> who boasts boast in the Lord." (1 Cor. 1:26–31)

Weakness as described by the New Testament writers is about people operating not out of their own skills, pedigree, background, education, or power but out of their suffering, dependency, and humility. Frequently, the Scriptures picture the people of God with images not of power but of smallness and in the hiddenness of weakness. Those who enjoyed the most dramatic manifestations of divine power were often those of the greatest humility (e.g., Abraham in Gen. 18:7; Moses in Ex. 3:11; David in 1 Sam. 18:23).

GOD-SHAPED BURDENS

There is a cliché I've heard in Christian circles that needs to be done away with. "God will never give you more than you can handle" is a phrase most of us say to each other when confronted with painful trials or suffering. I know what we mean when we say it; Paul writes in 1 Corinthians, "No temptation has overtaken you except what is common to mankind. And God is faithful; he will not let you be tempted beyond what you can bear. But when you are tempted, he will also provide a way out so that you can endure it" (1 Cor. 10:13).

While this is most certainly true, it is not quite the same thing as saying that God will never give us more than we can handle. In fact,

I think Scripture demonstrates just the opposite. God is all about giving us more than we can handle so that we'll actually have to trust Him. God is actively, passionately, and relentlessly about the business of giving us more than we can handle so that our power, wisdom, and strength will be brought to an end.

This is why Paul's teaching on weakness is so profound for the journey of faith. We think faith is supposed to protect us from being brought to a place of such desperation, but Paul suggests that faith *is* that point of desperation—that is the place where faith and trust in God actually begin.

But so much of American life and Christianity is designed precisely so that I never reach this point. I don't want to be weak; I want to be heroic, powerful, and important. I am conditioned (even in church!) to overcome obstacles, not embrace my limitations.

The point: God's desire is to work through human vulnerability rather than overcome it.

300?

Think about the biblical story of Gideon. It is told in the book of Judges, a series of narratives that follow a similar pattern: Israel disobeyed God; God allowed Israel to be disciplined by some outside force; Israel cried out for deliverance; God raised up a deliverer (or judge) to be the means of rescue; then the cycle began again.

In Gideon's time the Midianites had been oppressing the Israelites for seven years. God's angel appeared to Gideon while he was working and told him that the Lord was with him. A conversation ensued:

"Pardon me, my lord," Gideon replied, "but if the LORD is with us, why has all this happened to us? Where are all his wonders that our ancestors told us about when they said, 'Did not the LORD bring us up out of Egypt?' But now the LORD has abandoned us and given us into the hand of Midian."

The LORD turned to him and said, "Go in the strength you have and save Israel out of Midian's hand. Am I not sending you?"

"Pardon me, my lord," Gideon replied, "but how can I save Israel? My clan is the weakest in Manasseh, and I am the least in my family."

The LORD answered, "I will be with you, and you will strike down all the Midianites, leaving none alive." (Judg. 6:13–16)

What is interesting here is Gideon's response to God's summons. Like so many of the heroes of the faith, Gideon needed repeated assurances that God was indeed with him and would give him victory. Here is another example of God using the weak ("My clan is the weakest in Manasseh, and I am the least in my family") to shame the strong. God assured Gideon of His presence and Gideon proceeded to gather an army.

Thirty-three thousand Israelites gathered to war against Midian, but God insisted on fewer men.

The LORD said to Gideon, "You have too many men. I cannot deliver Midian into their hands, or

Israel would boast against me, 'My own strength has saved me.' Now announce to the army, 'Anyone who trembles with fear may turn back and leave Mount Gilead.'" So twenty-two thousand men left, while ten thousand remained.

But the LORD said to Gideon, "There are still too many men. Take them down to the water, and I will thin them out for you there. If I say, 'This one shall go with you,' he shall go; but if I say, 'This one shall not go with you,' he shall not go."

So Gideon took the men down to the water. There the LORD told him, "Separate those who lap the water with their tongues as a dog laps from those who kneel down to drink." Three hundred of them drank from cupped hands, lapping like dogs. All the rest got down on their knees to drink.

The LORD said to Gideon, "With the three hundred men that lapped I will save you and give the Midianites into your hands. Let all the others go home." So Gideon sent the rest of the Israelites home but kept the three hundred, who took over the provisions and trumpets of the others. (Judg. 7:2–8)

So God narrowed the number of fighting men from 33,000 to 300, and He did this so that Israel would not think its own strength saved them. He purposely gave them more than they could handle, bringing them to the place where He was the only hope of rescue and victory they had. Notice, this is the same rationale that Paul used when writing about how God uses the weak things to shame the strong—so that no one will boast before Him.

We think the story of Gideon is only a cute and quaint Sunday school story that works great on flannelgraphs, but it is far more than that. This is instructive as to the way God works in the life of faith. Far from keeping us from being overwhelmed, God often throws us in over our heads so that we'll look to Him for rescue and salvation. We misunderstand God's purposes in this. We are convinced He is most interested in keeping us safe, but that is not true. He is not after our safety; He is after our faith and our love, and to get both, He must expose us to risk and suffering. We'll never see His power if we refuse to have ours limited. God's way is not to take us out of trials, but to comfort us with His presence in the midst of them and to exchange our strength for His in the face of them. This is how God works out His purposes for the world—He puts treasure "in jars of clay to show that this all-surpassing power is from God and not from us" (2. Cor. 4:7). By our union with Christ in and through our weakness, we display God's glory.

It is to His greatness that He uses people like us; it is a testimony to His glory that He can take anything or anyone to be used for His purpose in the world. He shows His wisdom by using foolishness; He shows His strength by using weakness. God shows His true greatness by using the lowly and despised things of the world to bring out His purposes in human history. In His hands, our brokenness can be made beautiful.

He does this so that none of us live under the illusion that we ourselves are up for the task and boast before Him. He designs circumstances so that we are in over our heads and chooses unlikely people so that He gets the credit and glory. He brings us to the end of our sufficiency so that we'll rest in His. As I've said, we hate this. We don't want to learn this lesson *personally*. Perhaps that is why the church is so infatuated with tools, techniques, and marketing. When the pastor needs to be seen as an expert theologian, communicator, visionary, manager, administrator, recruiter, CEO, leader, coach, mentor, marriage counselor, and spiritual director ... it's easy to understand why there is so much burnout among the clerical ranks. If our churches don't embrace and visibly express weakness, what hope can there be for the rest of us? That is why it is completely antithetical to Jesus to rank churches based on how fast they are growing or how big they are. All this does is glorify and promote what our culture deems as strength, even though ranking, comparison, and pride are clearly weakness from God's point of view.

The American church has bought wholesale into the cultural assumptions of glory, power, and strength. One of the reasons our churches and ministries are so ineffective is because we don't make room for God's power, since we are so enamored with our own. We don't make room for weakness—everything in our churches has to be *excellent* and *well-produced*. So we schedule things by the minute, rehearse our transitions and prayers, seek out the next killer series or curriculum or program; and all the while Jesus has moved on to people who have *nothing* other than Him.

THE ANTI-AMERICAN DREAM

The most dangerous assumption we unknowingly accept about the American Dream is that our greatest asset is our own ability. This view says that if we work hard, believe in ourselves, and keep at it, we can do almost anything. The American Dream prizes what people can accomplish in their own power and to their own glory. The gospel, by contrast, beckons us to die to ourselves, to believe in God and trust in *His* power. God confronts us with our utter inability to accomplish anything of value apart from Him.

The American Dream is to make much of ourselves. The gospel is to make much of Jesus. God delights in exalting our inability; He intentionally puts His people in situations where they come face-to-face with their need for Him. Not just with Gideon, but with us, too. God is always looking for people who will trust His supernatural ability to turn ordinary people into vessels for His use. That is why the disciples were "unschooled, ordinary men" (Acts 4), and children were held up as examples of what greatness and faith look like in God's kingdom (Mark 10). That is why God chose an old barren woman and her elderly husband to give birth to a nation (Gen. 11—12) and the youngest of eight sons to be a king (1 Sam. 16).

God leads us to places where we don't know how He'll work or we can't see what He's up to. It is not God's way to give us formulas or blueprints. His will often makes sense only through the rearview mirror. God delights in calling us into places where faith grows more readily—where we are in over our heads or at the end of our ropes. He does this so we'll learn to trust Him, though we usually resist going where He takes us. The walls I hit in life train me to realize that I can't do it all. I actually need to rely on Jesus, or I'll be in trouble. This is a lesson we don't want to learn willingly. So God brings us to the end of things to teach us that weakness is actually strength when it causes us to live in brokenness and dependence upon Him.

The American Dream is to live in our strength; God's dream is that we live in our weakness. The one way of living is completely antithetical to the other. But if we really desire to see God move in mighty ways, to fully embrace the life that Jesus has for us, then we must be brought to the end of our power and strength. As Dallas Willard once said, the Christian life is what you do when you realize that you can do nothing.

THE NATURE OF FAITH (AND WHY WE DON'T LIKE IT)

Chapter 6

‖‖‖

FAITH DEMANDS MYSTERY

A couple of years ago I was sitting between Christmas Eve services at our church wondering why we needed to work so hard to celebrate the holiday. As a professional religious person, I feel pressure every Christmas to somehow make the stories that are so familiar to us seem new every time. The very familiarity we have with the Christmas story robs us of the ability to appreciate the mystery and wonder it should provoke. Why is it not enough at our Christmas services to simply just announce that the Word became flesh and walked among us? Why do I need all the props and traditions to "get in the mood"? Why do I have to work so hard to be amazed by what God has done?

At what point did most of us cease being amazed by God? When did we stop being astonished by who God is and what God has done?

We know that Mary was a virgin, that Caesar Augustus issued a decree, and that King Herod plotted against another "King of the Jews," although that king was born in a lowly place. We know the songs, stories, and traditions. So we stop paying attention. We quit really listening or thinking about what it is we celebrate. We cease looking for the small and usually unnoticed details. We sleepwalk through the season. And what is true of us in the Christmas season is just as true of us all year. We spend most of our lives on autopilot, and that is just the way we like it.

I have become convinced that one of the main projects of modern Christianity is to remove the mystery of biblical faith. We are far more comfortable with tips, steps, and techniques for living than we are with ruthlessly trusting the unpredictable God of the Bible. That is why God is so passionately committed to breaking the categories and boundaries we place on Him. Certainly He may (and does) place boundaries around Himself—when Jesus willingly took on the limitations of human flesh, for example. But when it comes to us, God is more about deepening the mystery of faith, not removing it. He wants to wake us up and calls us to pay more attention. Jesus should get bigger the longer we walk with Him. Life and faith should grow to be more profound and wondrous, not less.

M. Scott Peck has written about the stages in human spiritual development.[1] Peck argues that people are not all at the same place spiritually; there is a pattern of progression through identifiable stages in human spiritual life. I am not arguing for the truth of Peck's schema; I just want to use it to discuss the relationship between faith and mystery.

Peck identifies four stages of human spiritual development:

Stage 1—Chaotic and Antisocial

Peck suggests that every human being starts here, with an underdeveloped sense of spirituality. They are *chaotic* in that nothing governs them except the chaos of their desires and preferences. They are driven to exercise their will in almost exclusively self-gratifying ways, because there is no greater principle that they submit to. Peck labels this group *antisocial* because, he suggests, they are generally incapable of genuinely loving others. They may look loving and think of themselves that way, but their relationships are essentially manipulative and self-serving. They love others in order to love themselves.

Peck believes children and roughly 20 percent of adults are in this stage. Once those in stage one wake up to the chaos of their own inner lives (usually through pain), they begin to progress to the next stage.

Stage 2—Formal and Institutional

People run from the chaos of their inner lives by turning to something outside themselves that gives their lives meaning, structure, and purpose. They will look for the comfort and structure of an institution: prison life, the military, a career, or religion. That is why Peck calls this stage *institutional*. People at this stage look toward something structured *outside* of themselves for guidance and leadership.

This stage is also *formal* because most people in this stage become attached to the forms (as opposed to the essence) of religion (or whatever else they have turned to for help in governing their lives). They become attached to the liturgy, styles, and methods of the institution. Since it is precisely these forms that are responsible for their liberation from internal chaos, they may become defensive when these forms are changed. Peck suggests that the majority of churchgoers fall into this category.

Peck argues that people in this stage view God almost exclusively as an external, transcendent being; they have very little understanding of the immanent God. While many consider God to be loving, they also believe that He will punish those who break the rules. It is no accident that God is pictured as the giant "police officer" in the sky, because that is precisely the kind of God they need; just as they need the legalisms of religion for their governance. *Stability* is a principle value for people in this stage, but over time they begin to internalize the principles and practices of religion and become less dependent on the institution for leadership. Some begin to question the forms and institutions that brought about their deliverance from chaos. At this point they begin the transition to stage three.

Stage 3—Skeptical and Individual

People enter this stage when they begin to question the institutions and forms that had previously brought comfort and stability. Although they are frequently considered nonbelievers, Peck holds that people in this stage are generally more spiritually developed than many content to stay in stage two. They are *individualistic* in that they are less inclined to accept the authority of the institution and more desirous to find out for themselves the truth of their beliefs. Although individualistic, these people are not antisocial. They are deeply committed to other people and causes once they have wrestled through their questions. These people are more *skeptical* than they were in stage two. They question everything and need to make up their own minds. They are active truth seekers, and if they keep asking and seeking long enough, they begin to see there was something to stage-two beliefs. At that point, they begin the journey into the next stage.

Stage 4—Mystical and Communal

Peck sees people in this stage as *communal*, not because they live in communities, but because among human beings they are the ones most aware of the underlying connectedness and unity between all things and people. They see human society as a whole instead of in separate and antagonistic subfactions. Peck labels people here as *mystical* because they are comfortable with mystery. Mystics acknowledge the enormity of the unknown, but rather than being frightened by it, they seek to move deeper into it. They realize that the more they understand, the greater the mystery will become.

People in this stage are attracted to mystery, which distinguishes them markedly from those in stage two. Those in stage two need simple, clear-cut answers and dogmatic structures, and have little appetite for the unknown and the mysterious. Peck argues that while stage-four people will enter religion in order to approach mystery, in stage two, people enter religion to *escape* from it. Thus we have people entering (and participating in) the same church, denomination, or religion from totally opposite motives.

FAITH AS MYSTERY

Peck is quick to suggest that there are many gradations within and between the four stages. Someone may enter stage three but find stage-two belief more comfortable, so they bounce back and forth between the two. He also points out that there exists a sense of threat among people in different stages of religious development. It is my observation that we are mostly threatened by the people in the stages beyond us. Stage-one people are threatened by just about everything and everyone (though they may often look like they have everything together on the outside). Stage-two people view stage-one people as hopeless "sinners" but are very much threatened by stage-three people, who are skeptics, and by the stage-four people, who seem to believe in the same sort of things they do but believe with a freedom the stage-two people find absolutely terrifying. Stage-three people are intimidated by stage-four people, who are open and thoughtful but who have bought into all the "God" stuff.

Again, whether or not Peck's analysis is correct is beside the point. What is interesting is the insight that people can come to religious belief from one of two opposite perspectives: moving toward mystery or moving away from it. For some, the wonder and mystery of human life is what *draws* us to faith; for others, religion should provide the clarity and answers to the big questions of life; it should remove mystery not reinforce it.

My guess is that many American Christians fall into the second category—Christianity is supposed to alleviate mystery, paradox, and tension, not amplify it. I certainly am sympathetic to that desire. I would like my questions about evil or predestination distilled into one-minute sound bites. I prefer three easy steps to knowing God's will rather than wrestling through the risk of making a decision and trusting God for the results.

But God seems to have another agenda. There is no question that God speaks a clear and authoritative word to humankind through

Jesus of Nazareth. I simply wish to point out that, at times, the same impulse that drives us (in chemistry, astrophysics, medicine) to understand and master our world drives us also (in theology) to force biblical faith in the biblical God into categories and structures that, by definition, attempt to remove mystery, tension, and paradox. This is not wholly a bad thing. God does call us to love Him with our minds. I love theology and see it as necessary. But I want to balance us. God does speak to us through creation, conscience, and the Scriptures. But often His speaking raises more questions than it answers. And that is how it should be.

MY NAME IS YHWH

Names are important in Western culture. Parents choose names for their children after much thought and discussion. For the rest of a person's life, he or she is identified by the name they were given at birth. But the significance of names in our day cannot compare with the significance of names in biblical times. Ancient peoples understood that a name expressed the essence or identity of a person. It was far more than a label. According to Proverbs 22:1, "A good name is more desirable than great riches." In the biblical world, a good name meant more than even a good reputation, because it identified the character of the person carrying it.

When Westerners give names, we don't attach those names to something intrinsic to the person; they serve only as identifiers. My name is Mike, but it could have just as easily been Benjamin or Larry. There is no inherent "Mike-ness" about me that my name reflects. I'm Mike, but that doesn't tell you anything about me. My parents didn't lay hands on me and prophesy that I was going to have a "Mike" kind of existence and that is why they named me the way they did. It was just a tag, a way of identifying me that was not attached to anything intrinsic to me or my character.

The Jewish process of naming is much different. Places were named on the basis of whatever significant events had occurred there. People were named as expressions of character or destiny. Names revealed something about their bearer. That was why they were viewed as significant. You could never separate the essence of a person or place from its name. At times, God would change a person's name to signify their changing character or destiny (e.g., Abram to Abraham; Jacob to Israel; Simon to Peter).

Names are distinguished from titles. Titles are formal; names are informal. Names express familiarity, relationship, and intimacy. In conversation, we often move from calling someone by their title to calling them by their name. I have many titles—pastor, author, father, and husband—but only one name. My wife doesn't call me "fellow taxpayer" or "fellow citizen" when she addresses me, she calls me "Mike" or, if I am in trouble, "Michael."

This background is necessary to understand why God's name is a big deal in the Scriptures. God had many titles, but His name was given to Moses in Exodus 3.

To know and use God's name meant one understood something of His essential character and being, that one could identify and understand (know) Him. But God is the sovereign Creator of the universe. God existed before anyone or anything. Only God can understand His being enough to name Himself, and He alone has the authority to do it. It was Moses who finally had the courage to ask God to give Himself a name. In the book of Exodus, Moses said to God, "Suppose I go to the Israelites and say to them, 'The God of your fathers has sent me to you,' and they ask me, 'What is his name?' Then what shall I tell them?" (Exod. 3:13). God answered Moses by revealing His name:

> God said to Moses, "I AM WHO I AM. [Or I WILL BE WHAT I WILL BE.] This is what you are to say to the Israelites: 'I AM has sent me to you.'"
>
> God also said to Moses, "Say to the Israelites, 'The LORD, the God of your fathers—the God of Abraham, the God of Isaac and the God of Jacob— has sent me to you.'
>
> "This is my name forever,
>> the name you shall call me
>> from generation to generation." (Exod. 3:14–15)

Three variations of God's name are used in this passage. The first one, "I AM WHO I AM" is the Hebrew phrase, *Ehyeh asher Ehyeh*, which can also be translated, "I WILL BE WHAT I WILL BE." *Ehyeh* is the imperfect first-person form of the verb *havah*, which is translated, "I will be."

The second one is mentioned immediately after the first, "I AM has sent me to you." "I AM" is simply *Ehyeh* by itself; it is God's shortened name when He speaks of Himself in the first person.

Last, God gives the name that the Israelites are to use when referring to Him in the third person. He taught them to say "Yahweh"—"He WILL BE" (not "I WILL BE").

So God's full name is "I AM WHO I AM," which essentially means, "I exist. I am dependent on nothing whatsoever for My existence. I am sheer sufficiency." God shortens the name to "I AM" when He refers to Himself but commanded the Israelites to use the third-person form of "I AM"—"He IS"—when calling Him by name. When God speaks of Himself, He says "I AM," and when we speak of Him, we say, "He IS."

This name ("He IS") is the most-often-used noun in the Hebrew scriptures. It occurs over 6,800 times. In Hebrew texts it is spelled only with consonants: *Y-H-W-H*, and it is called the Four-Letter name—or tetragrammaton in Greek. Rabbinic Judaism refers to it as *haShem*—literally, "The Name." In biblical times YHWH was spoken with accompanying vowel sounds. But sometime prior to the first century, that pronunciation was gradually suppressed out of reverence for God's name, so we are not quite sure how it was pronounced.

BACK TO MOSES

The religious climate of Moses's day (remember, he was raised in Egypt) was that there were many gods and goddesses—deities that governed the crops, the stars, the Nile River—almost every facet of human life had a god/goddess attached to it. These deities had names that revealed a little bit of who they were and what they did. One needed to know the "name" of the god or goddess to properly worship and offer sacrifice so the deity would work on their behalf. Moses had been trained in Pharaoh's household, and he had been trained to learn the names of all the gods. And he was trained and versed in what each of these gods would do for him.

So asking for God's name was a natural question for Moses to ask. I love what God said in response, however. When God gave Moses His name, it was like God was saying, "In contrast to all the pretender gods of Egypt, I actually exist. I actually *am*. I'm real." God didn't explain Himself or defend Himself—He just said, "This is My name forever."

God answered Moses's question and gave Moses His name but did it in a way that conveyed mystery, wonder, and awe. Calling God by His name is more intimate than calling God by a title, but the name we are given is a reminder that God is different from us, and He can never be figured out. His name is both an invitation to covenantal relationship *and* a reminder that He is mysterious, holy, and awesome. As the people of God, we must hold to both sides of this tension. God can be known in and through Jesus, but He can never be fully figured out. The church has erred both in making Jesus too human *and* in making Him not human enough. He speaks, but His speaking doesn't remove mystery; in this case it increases it.

In the New Testament, as the good news of Jesus moved beyond its Jewish context, the writers of the Scriptures were forced to use Greek words and concepts that would help Greek audiences understand God's work in and through Jesus. Often they would use generic words for "God." One of the most famous examples of this is in John 3:16, where John recorded Jesus saying, "For God so loved the world …" YHWH, God's covenantal name, isn't used here; the Greek word *theos* is used instead. *Theos* is a generic proper noun that was used to denote a god or gods. It is very similar to the English word *god*. If you take *god* and look it up in the dictionary, here is what you get: "any of various beings conceived of as supernatural, immortal, and having special powers over the lives and affairs of people and the course of nature." God had revealed Himself to Israel as YHWH, but the writers of the Scriptures were looking for a word, because they wanted their Greek audience to understand who this God was. They couldn't adequately communicate YHWH to a Greek audience, so they took the word for *god* and made it into GOD—the one true God.

What developed from the word *theos* is the word *theology*, which is the study of God. God and His revelation about Himself became subjects of classrooms, lectures, and syllabi. All of this is incredibly important. But if our study of God does not lead us to the worship of God, we're in trouble. It is possible to write papers, pass exams, and memorize facts about God but still not know YHWH and His Son, Jesus. We can often dissect and debate God as if being *right* about Him is more important than being *in love* with Him. Maybe it is; but the goal of knowing about Him is to love Him. You shouldn't have one without the other. Theology can be used to make God bigger, but it can also be used to make God smaller.

We know this mistake is possible, of course, and that is part of the problem. Part of the reason why there is a tragic lack of wonder, awe, and astonishment in our churches is because we think we already know all there is to know. Every Christmas I have to convince people they don't know the Christmas story; every Easter I have to persuade people that they don't fully comprehend the Easter story. When I teach on prayer, obedience, evangelism, or the parables, the first thing I have to do is overcome the initial thought most of us have: *I've heard this before. I know that verse. I know where this is going.* How sad would it be if the people of God lost the sense of discovery and wonder and pursuit that Jesus desires? God explained and expressed Himself as YHWH and His Son, Jesus, as the personal Creator of the universe who wants to enter into relationship with us. The problem is that people get sidetracked with the study of Him and fail to realize that God cannot fit inside their particular brain.

What drives our study of God is the realization that there is so much we don't know. Mystery is what fuels our worship—the paradox of knowing God but never reaching the point where we've got Him figured out. Good teaching needs to raise questions and give people things to ponder and wrestle with instead of always wrapping everything up in a pretty red Christian bow. The danger is that we get to the point where we think we know all already, so we quit pursuing God and lose our sense of amazement. We must allow the questions that the Bible poses about God to grow more vast and wondrous. There are a peace and a joy that come from understanding that though you can know God, you'll never be able to figure Him out.

Please understand, theology is a good thing. I am a *big* fan. It is central to the life of faith. But it is only the *basis* for faith, not faith itself. We must constantly be reminded that whatever view of God we have it is not big enough or good enough or true enough. No matter how high our view of God, the reality of Him is bigger and better.

FACEDOWN

In the Scriptures even people who had very high views of God were staggered by His presence when they actually saw Him.

Job was the most righteous man on the earth during his time. The book that bears his name is about how God allowed His enemy to wreak havoc over Job's life. Job didn't understand why any of his suffering was happening, and he moved back and forth between accusing and questioning God and trusting that God was still at work in his life. God appeared at the very end of the book (in a whirlwind!), and afterward Job said:

> I know that you can do all things;
>> no purpose of yours can be thwarted.
> You asked, "Who is this that obscures my plans
>> without knowledge?"
>> Surely I spoke of things I did not understand,
>> things too wonderful for me to know.
>
> You said, "Listen now, and I will speak;
>> I will question you,
>> and you shall answer me."
> My ears had heard of you
>> but now my eyes have seen you.
> Therefore I despise myself
>> and repent in dust and ashes. (Job 42:2–6)

Job's response was humility and repentance, an appreciation for how vast and awesome God is. I love what he said: "My ears had heard of you but now my eyes have seen you." He had a view of God that turned out to be too small and too safe. All his beliefs about God were smashed into tiny pieces when confronted with the reality of the living God of Israel, YHWH.

John, one of Jesus's closest disciples and author of one of the accounts of Jesus that present Him in the most exalted terms, upon seeing the risen and glorified Jesus, fell down before Him in holy fear. John wrote about this encounter with the Jesus he had eaten with and walked with and talked with for years:

> I turned around to see the voice that was speaking to me. And when I turned I saw seven golden lampstands, and among the lampstands was someone like a son of man, dressed in a robe reaching down to his feet and with a golden sash around his chest. The hair on his head was white like wool, as white as snow, and his eyes were like blazing fire. His feet were like bronze glowing in a furnace, and his voice was like the sound of rushing waters. In his right hand he held seven stars, and coming out of his mouth was a sharp, double-edged sword. His face was like the sun shining in all its brilliance.
>
> When I saw him, I fell at his feet as though dead. Then he placed his right hand on me and said: "Do not be afraid. I am the First and the Last." (Rev. 1:12–17)

No matter what view of God we have, it's not big enough. John and Job had a high view of God, but His reality left them both speechless and in awe. Our problem is that in nice, neat consumeristic America, we want God to do things that make sense, and *then* we'll worship Him. We have made a God out of our intellects and want to worship a God who doesn't offend our moral or intellectual sensibilities.

God revealed Himself, though, as a God whom we will never figure out. Yes, we can know Him intimately. "For God so loved the world ..." The basic elements of the gospel are easily understood by anyone. The smallest child can say yes to Jesus and enter His kingdom. And yet we can ponder John 3:16 for the rest of our lives and never get to the bottom of it. So we are left with the mystery of the God who can be known but never completely understood. He has spoken but hasn't answered all our questions. He has revealed Himself but only enough for us to know that He is good and holy in a way that is far beyond us.

Chapter 7

FAITH DEMANDS DESPERATION

I used to hate preaching on Easter Sunday. I know that sounds a bit bad for a pastor to say, but it's true. I have always felt quite a bit of pressure come Easter-time to put together a meaningful and relevant Easter celebration that meets the expectations of those who will come. Loads of people who do not attend church regularly show up Easter Sunday, and very often the friends and family inviting them to our church will approach me to let me know their "unsaved" friends are coming (with the not-so-subtle message being "You'd better not screw it up!"). So I find myself, year after year, feeling the need to find some unique and compelling "angle" on the Easter story. I think that if I do a "good job," maybe these visitors will come back next week. So I, and many others like me, put a ton of pressure on ourselves to put our best foot forward. We market all our ministries and marriage enrichment courses, all in the hope that someone will have a positive experience and return to our church community. Easter can turn into less of a celebration of the risen Jesus and more of a promotional event for God and our church.

We try to convince people that God is good and worth following. We do this by trying to attract them to our churches. Some in our area even give prizes away on Easter to those who attend for the first time. (One church offered a drawing for a new car.) Part of me is very sympathetic to this—we do want as many people as possible to come to know Jesus, and we'll do anything to make that happen.

But I still can't shake the feeling that something is tragically wrong with this approach. Perhaps, we're actually doing Jesus a disservice the more we try to make Him attractive.

It's like God Himself isn't compelling enough, so we have to add some programming, felt-needs ministry, and slick and relevant teaching to really get the point across. If that doesn't work, we'll market the benefits of following Jesus: if you accept Him, you'll go to heaven; you'll never be alone; you'll be healthy and wealthy; the Jesus-shaped hole in your heart will be full; you'll find meaning, significance, and purpose. If you accept Him, He'll throw in some steak knives.

It's like one big infomercial for Jesus.

And maybe all of that is true—except for the knives.

Maybe we'll find all those things.

But that's still not enough to build a life of faith on. Because in my experience, following Jesus often makes things *harder*, not easier; *more confusing*, not less confusing; and more aware of all the brokenness, pain, and suffering in the world. Jesus raises more questions than He answers. He calls us to live by faith, not by sight, and that means we live with ambiguity, mystery, and tension.

This means that our marketing pieces may need a bit of an overhaul.

What is the reward of following Jesus?

Jesus.

Jesus is the reward of following Jesus. That's it. Nothing else.

Until we actually believe that, we'll be tempted to settle for programs, felt needs, and offering free cars. Until we believe that *He* is the reward, the treasure, and the point, we'll continue to preach a gospel that is focused only on the forgiveness of my sins and my entrance into heaven when I die. Certainly there are benefits for us following Jesus, and eternal life is foremost among them, but they are not the point.

So much of our marketing of Jesus to the world consists in listing the benefits of following Him, but this only conditions people to be in it for what they get out of it. Jesus Himself is the reward we are to treasure; everything else is a bonus. If Jesus Himself isn't enough for someone, then felt-needs marketing won't ultimately matter. The means you use to attract people to Jesus are the same means you must use to keep them. If appealing to the consumer benefits of following Jesus is used to attract people to Him, what happens when Jesus no longer cooperates?

JESUS AND FOCUS GROUPS

What makes all the pressure I feel even more maddening is that Jesus never talked about Himself or God's kingdom in these ways. He never begged or bribed anyone into His movement. He spent little time addressing felt needs or selling the benefits of followership. He described what God and His kingdom were like and called people to faith and repentance. He confronted His contemporaries with the reckless and relentless love of the God He called Father and the call to trusting obedience that lies at the heart of biblical faith. We spend a lot of time making promises about how things are going to go once people follow Jesus, as if we think we have to dazzle them into His kingdom. But you never see any of this with Jesus Himself.

If He came across someone who had other options, Jesus *let them walk away.* He didn't force or manipulate anyone. He didn't bait and switch. And often, when His popularity threatened to drown out His real mission, He would offer a hard teaching or warn people about the *cost* of following Him. In essence, He would scare them away. Consider:

> Anyone who loves their father or mother more than me is not worthy of me; anyone who loves their son or daughter more than me is not worthy of me. (Matt. 10:37)

> Large crowds were traveling with Jesus, and turning to them he said: "If anyone comes to me and does not hate father and mother, wife and children, brothers and sisters—yes, even their own life—such a person cannot be my disciple. And whoever does not carry their cross and follow me cannot be my disciple." (Luke 14:25–27)

Not exactly the stuff we preach when we are trying to make Jesus attractive to people on Easter Sunday.

Jesus didn't seem to suffer at all from the need to please the crowds or dazzle them into His service (wasn't that one of Satan's temptations of Jesus—to dazzle the crowds with miracles?). He refused to perform miracles on demand and warned many not to tell others who He was. He was content with His own obscurity for the vast majority of His life.

During this time, He wasn't lonely or hurting for worship. During Jesus's entry into Jerusalem, many in the crowd were shouting prayers and singing psalms. A fascinating exchange ensues:

> When he came near the place where the road goes down the Mount of Olives, the whole crowd of disciples began joyfully to praise God in loud voices for all the miracles they had seen:
>
> "Blessed is the king who comes in the name of the Lord!"
>
> "Peace in heaven and glory in the highest!"
>
> Some of the Pharisees in the crowd said to Jesus, "Teacher, rebuke your disciples!"
>
> "I tell you," he replied, "if they keep quiet, the stones will cry out." (Luke 19:37–40)

Jesus wasn't lonely or insecure. He felt no pressure to polish up His message to make it more palatable to the crowds. The whole earth declared the glory of His Father and the stones were just wait-ing for a chance to celebrate Him. He wasn't worried about His poll numbers or the slander by His opponents. He simply embodied and announced the proximity of God's kingdom on earth and sum-moned all to repentance. He gave everyone the opportunity to come or the opportunity to walk away.

DESPERATE FAITH

There was one particular response from the crowds that drew Jesus's attention more than any other. Jesus came across all kinds of people: rich and poor, Jew and Gentile, male and female, clean and unclean. He loved all of them equally but responded to each based on how they responded to Him. Jesus was most responsive to *desperate* people—those who were brokenhearted or, in Jesus's words, who were "poor in spirit." Jesus responded to them with healing, grace, and mercy. To those who weren't as desperate, who had other options, Jesus responded differently. He didn't beg, bribe, or attempt to dazzle them into His kingdom. If they were unwilling to turn away from what ultimately would keep them from devotion to Him, He let them walk away.

Consider Jesus's response to a blind man:

> As Jesus approached Jericho, a blind man was sitting by the roadside begging. When he heard the crowd going by, he asked what was happening. They told him, "Jesus of Nazareth is passing by."
>
> He called out, "Jesus, Son of David, have mercy on me!"

> Those who led the way rebuked him and told
> him to be quiet, but he shouted all the more, "Son
> of David, have mercy on me!"
>
> Jesus stopped and ordered the man to be
> brought to him. When he came near, Jesus asked
> him, "What do you want me to do for you?"
>
> "Lord, I want to see," he replied.
>
> Jesus said to him, "Receive your sight; your
> faith has healed you." (Luke 18:35–42)

I love what the blind man did in response to those who told him to be quiet; the text says "but he shouted all the more." That man didn't care if he was mocked or ridiculed. He was at the end of his rope and calling out to Jesus was all he could think to do. And what did Jesus do in response? Jesus stopped and healed him.

I find that some religious people are uncomfortable with this kind of desperation. Desperate people are messy people; and messy people don't care to follow our religious conventions. I sometimes wonder if our churches aren't more like those who told the beggar to shut up. I wonder how our churches would handle someone twenty hours sober who came and interrupted a worship service—would such a person be told to shut up? Or would they be welcomed and encouraged to *shout all the more*? Jesus, evidently, didn't have any issue with those who weren't into religious propriety.

Another example:

> While Jesus was in one of the towns, a man came
> along who was covered with leprosy. When he saw

Jesus, he fell with his face to the ground and begged him, "Lord, if you are willing, you can make me clean."

Jesus reached out his hand and touched the man. "I am willing," he said. "Be clean!" And immediately the leprosy left him. (Luke 5:12–13)

The social stigma accompanying leprosy in the first century was almost as debilitating as the disease itself. Lepers were cast out of community life. They were forced to live apart from everyone else. They were never touched and had to warn others of their coming by shouting, "Unclean! Unclean!" They were avoided and unable to participate in any aspect of community life. You can hear the brokenness of the man in his request of Jesus. There weren't many in ancient Israel who were considered less fortunate or less desirable than a man like this.

How did Jesus respond? By *touching* the man! We know Jesus didn't have to touch him in order to heal him; at other times, He healed by just speaking a word. So the touching was intentional. This would have been striking to Jesus's audience because it was thought that anything *unclean* infected anything *clean*; Jesus reversed this and demonstrated that His purity cleansed anything impure. His touch healed the man's leprosy. This was true morally and physically. And it is still true today. The touch of Jesus removes any impurity.

I wish to point you again to the way Jesus responded to someone "poor in spirit." A blind man interrupted a procession and Jesus stopped and healed. A leper fell to the ground and begged, and Jesus touched him. A woman who had a bleeding problem fought through a crowd just to touch the hem of Jesus's robe. Four men dug through the roof of a house to lower their paralyzed friend in front of Jesus. A notoriously sinful woman interrupted a dinner party to weep over Jesus's feet and wipe them with her hair. In each case, Jesus welcomed the disruption such people caused and responded to them with grace and mercy.

Time and again the desperate, the needy, the messy, and the crippled interrupted Jesus for His blessing. And Jesus responded the same way every time. He welcomed them. He healed them. He blessed and forgave them. There was something about their desperate faith that He responded to.

But when Jesus encountered folks who had other options, who had not yet decided that they'd do anything just to be near Jesus, He responded differently:

> As they were walking along the road, a man said to him, "I will follow you wherever you go."
>
> Jesus replied, "Foxes have dens and birds have nests, but the Son of Man has no place to lay his head."
>
> He said to another man, "Follow me."
>
> But he replied, "Lord, first let me go and bury my father."
>
> Jesus said to him, "Let the dead bury their own dead, but you go and proclaim the kingdom of God."
>
> Still another said, "I will follow you, Lord; but first let me go back and say goodbye to my family."
>
> Jesus replied, "No one who puts a hand to the plow and looks back is fit for service in the kingdom of God." (Luke 9:57–62)

These are very Jewish interactions that our cultural background may cause us to misunderstand. In each case, however, Jesus sought to clarify the urgency needed to follow Him. Again, He wasn't begging or bribing people; He wanted them to understand exactly what following Him demanded. In the first century, one's family was the basis of identity and obligation. It would be unthinkable to turn one's back on one's loved ones for any reason, yet that is what Jesus called His disciples to do. He said that one's family obligations were *secondary* to those of His kingdom. This would have been incredibly offensive to first-century hearers.

Another example:

> A certain ruler asked him, "Good teacher, what must I do to inherit eternal life?"
>
> "Why do you call me good?" Jesus answered. "No one is good—except God alone. You know the commandments: 'You shall not commit adultery, you shall not murder, you shall not steal, you shall not give false testimony, honor your father and mother.'"
>
> "All these I have kept since I was a boy," he said.
>
> When Jesus heard this, he said to him, "You still lack one thing. Sell everything you have and give to the poor, and you will have treasure in heaven. Then come, follow me."
>
> When he heard this, he became very sad, because he was very wealthy. Jesus looked at him and said, "How hard it is for the rich to enter the

kingdom of God! Indeed, it is easier for a camel to go through the eye of a needle than for someone who is rich to enter the kingdom of God." (Luke 18:18–25)

Mark's account of this story says that Jesus looked at the rich man "and loved him." The point for our purposes is that Jesus loved him, *but let the man walk away.* He didn't negotiate with the rich man or soften the invitation; He didn't beg or bribe. He clarified the nature of followership and let the rich man choose. Jesus seemed remarkably free from the pressure so many of His followers feel today to dress Him up and make Him more attractive.

To the people falling facedown, digging through roofs, and fighting through crowds, Jesus offered healing and mercy. But to the people hedging their bets, taking half steps, and exploring their options, Jesus insisted they abandon anything and everything that would get in the way of following Him. The most powerful stuff happens when we run out of options. So Jesus doesn't dazzle the crowds; He thins them out (e.g., John 6)!

BOX SEATS AT CHURCH?

Several years ago, my wife and I attended a Los Angeles Lakers game with some friends. Though we live close to L.A., we haven't yet jumped on the Lakers bandwagon. But this was too good to miss. We watched the game from one of the luxury suites that sits above the court. My friend drove us up to the private entrance and elevator at the Staples Center that is reserved for VIPs. Our suite was equipped with multiple flat-screen TVs, a free buffet, and eight seats that overlooked center court. I'll go to a Lakers game anytime with a deal like that. I didn't drive, didn't pay, and didn't leave hungry.

Everything has to be just right for me to go to a Lakers game. I want good seats, I don't want to fight traffic, and it matters who they are playing. I'm not like diehard Lakers fans who will follow the team for years whether or not the team is playing well or they have good seats. It doesn't matter to them if they have to park a mile away from the arena. They are committed to the team no matter what.

I am a lot like many of the people who fill our churches; I'll only show up if everything is just right. For those folks, the music and the teaching have to be good, the kids have to like the child-care program, and the service can't be too long. There should be ample parking, and the service times should be convenient.

The problem is that if I have to talk people into making a decision for Christ, I'll also have to talk them into keeping their commitment, convincing them it's in their best interests to do so.

Meanwhile, there are people across the world who will walk several miles, often meeting in the middle of nowhere, without seats and air-conditioning, for the privilege of worshipping Jesus with a dozen other believers. Others will meet in secret, under the threat of persecution and imprisonment, to pray and worship for hours without amplification or PowerPoint lyrics.

The difference between a casual fan and a diehard fan is similar to the difference between those who are desperate for Jesus and those who are not. It shouldn't matter who is teaching or what songs are sung as long as Jesus is honored and celebrated. Jesus isn't interested in people who will follow Him only if everything is just right. He loves us regardless, of course. But let's not delude ourselves into thinking that the casual approach many take to following Jesus is true discipleship. He isn't lucky to have us. He's not blessed by our weekly attendance at a ninety-minute worship service; He doesn't need the twenty dollars we throw into the offering plate. There are people dying for their faith around the world. People in the poorest parts of the world gather together in the face of opposition without coffee or convenient parking.

I once heard Francis Chan say that the book of Acts was his least favorite book of the Bible, because rarely can anyone in America read the account of the birth and expansion of the early church and say, "Wow, that is just like my church." Because the disparity between the early church and the twenty-first–century American church is so great, we have to resign ourselves to the idea that "that was then" and come up with reasons why that stuff doesn't happen today. Francis made the point that the early church was unstoppable—in the face of persecution, torture, imprisonment, it continued to grow. Nothing could stop it. But the church today is very stoppable. Just change the service times or worship styles or teaching methods, and people will church shop elsewhere. We've lost any sense of desperation that it all hinges on Jesus and that unless He shows up we're done for.

BURIED TREASURE

I love working with college students. They are refreshingly honest and passionate. I remember one conversation (that has since been repeated many times) where a young man was torn between having fun (the kind involving alcohol and sex) and following Jesus. His idea was to have fun now and get serious about Jesus later, when he settled down. He wondered what my thoughts were.

I remember thinking about what Jesus would say. Would Jesus try to convince the young man that following Him was the best way to have fun? Would Jesus talk to him about the costs of drinking and sexual sin? Or would Jesus love him and let him walk away? I was reminded of the picture Jesus gives in Matthew 13 of what coming into His kingdom is like: "The kingdom of heaven is like treasure hidden in a field. When a man found it, he hid it again, and then in his joy went and sold all he had and bought that field" (Matt. 13:44). In Jesus's day, of course, there weren't safety-deposit boxes or 401(k)s. The average family would have had valuable cloth or jewelry that had been handed down from generation to generation that would have to be hidden in order to be protected from theft. Sometimes, the treasure would be forgotten or the location of its hiding place lost. Jesus used the image of a worker in a field who discovered such a cache that was so valuable he liquidated everything he owned in order to purchase the field and thereby possess the treasure.

He did this with *great joy*, because he recognized the great value of what he'd found. This wasn't someone complaining about the demand to sell everything or lamenting all he could have had elsewhere. He was single-minded in pursuit. Unless we see Jesus and His kingdom as the treasure, following Him will seem burdensome and costly. As long as we believe there is treasure elsewhere, we'll pursue *that* instead of Christ. This is what the college student was wrestling with. He wasn't convinced that Jesus was really the treasure.

Jesus didn't dazzle people or list the benefits one would accrue by following Him. He just threw open the gates of His upside-down kingdom and looked for hearts that were open. If someone had other options, He would let them go to pursue their treasure elsewhere. He wasn't interested in being added to someone's preexisting agenda; He wanted His followers to pursue Him with single-minded devotion (and *joy!*) that would characterize a man who discovered treasure hidden in a field.

This was true in the first century for rich young rulers, and it's no less true for college students today. I may not be able to sing the very popular worship song that says "I'm desperate for you" with much integrity, but I am desperate *to be desperate* (though singing those words doesn't fit the melody of the song). I want to get to the place where I would fall down and beg or shout all the more or dig through a roof just to be close to Jesus.

And there, in those desperate places, Jesus does some of His best work.

Chapter 8

|||||||||||||||||||||||||||||||||||||||||||||||||||||||||||||||||||||||||||||||||||||||

FAITH DEMANDS SURRENDER

I'd like to think God relates to people the same way Santa Claus does. There are naughty people, who receive judgment and smiting, while nice people receive blessings and good gifts. God is always checking His list of who is naughty and who is nice. God rewards the nice and punishes the naughty. Simple, right?

But in the Scriptures the opposite is often true. Good and faithful people often have lives of sorrow and disappointment while wicked and unrighteous people seem to receive God's blessing. The Bible record raises both questions: Why do bad things happen to good people and why do good things happen to bad people?

As it turns out, faithfulness to God is no guarantee of a life of what we normally (and sometimes falsely) call blessing. Which pretty much shoots holes in any view of the life of faith that says God promises to make us healthy and wealthy in return for our faith.

It is possible to do all that God asks of you and still have your life fall apart.

Take John the Baptist, for instance. John and Jesus were cousins, born six months apart. John always seemed to have an idea of who Jesus really was, far before anyone else. For the first time in four hundred years, a prophetic voice was heard again in Israel. John was that voice. Luke says that John reacted in utero to the presence of Jesus. At the beginning of Jesus's ministry, John announced that Jesus was the Lamb of God, chosen to take away the sins of the world. John balked at the thought of baptizing Jesus out of respect for the authority Jesus carried. In short, John was fully aware of who Jesus was.

All of this makes John's question to Jesus in Matthew 11 all the more strange. John, while in prison, sent some of his disciples to Jesus with the following question: "Are you the one who is to come, or should we expect someone else?" (Matt. 11:3).

Some think that John was expressing doubts about Jesus's messiahship, since much of Jesus's ministry didn't line up with John's pronouncement of judgment over Israel (e.g., Luke 3:7–9). The grace and mercy of Jesus, the story goes, didn't line up with John's expectations of what the Messiah would do. But I'm not so sure.

"The one to come" is an obscure reference to the coming messianic king in Zechariah 9. First-century Jews often employed a common method of discussion called *Remez* (also called the hinting method), where a part of a passage could be quoted but the whole context was in view. They would quote a verse in part that would immediately draw the minds of the audience to not only the actual words quoted but also the entire passage in which they were recorded. This was a shorthand method of discussion that hinted at the whole context of a passage while using only a portion of a verse.

We could do a similar thing with some well-known passages of the Bible. If, in discussion, I made a point about the Lord being my shepherd, most listeners would know that to be a reference to Psalm 23 and the rest of its context. I could just mention the first line, and the rest of the passage would be understood.

Some think this is what John is doing in his discussion with Jesus. The *Remez* is the phrase "the one to come." Jesus would have known the reference, as well as the fact that two verses later, the prophet speaks of the coming king bringing freedom to prisoners. So I think John was asking, in a very Jewish way, if Jesus was going to set him free from prison.

Jesus's reply reinforces this interpretation:

> Jesus replied, "Go back and report to John what you hear and see: The blind receive sight, the lame walk, those who have leprosy are cleansed, the deaf hear, the dead are raised, and the good news is proclaimed to the poor. Blessed is anyone who does not stumble on account of me." (Matt. 11:4–6)

Jesus combined two passages in his response to John. The first is from Isaiah 35:

> Then will the eyes of the blind be opened
> and the ears of the deaf unstopped.
> Then will the lame leap like a deer,
> and the mute tongue shout for joy
> (Isa. 35:5–6)

The second is from Isaiah 61:

> The Spirit of the Sovereign LORD is on me,
>> because the LORD has anointed me
>> to proclaim good news to the poor.
> He has sent me to bind up the brokenhearted,
>> to proclaim freedom for the captives
>> and release from darkness for the prisoners.
>> (Isa. 61:1)

Both of these passages were well-known messianic passages, and John would have had them memorized. What is interesting for our purposes is to notice what Jesus included and what He left out. Jesus left out the part from Isaiah 61 about "proclaiming freedom for the captives and release from darkness for the prisoners." There was no reason for this exclusion unless John were inquiring about his release from prison.

This understanding is further affirmed by what Jesus included instead. He added, "Blessed is anyone who does not stumble on account of me." Again, there was no reason for Him to include this unless He was saying, in effect, "Yes, John, I am the one to come, but you are not getting out of prison." That was why He added the blessing to the one who doesn't fall away. And sure enough, John was beheaded in prison relatively soon after.

Does God always give us what we want? We would like Him to, wouldn't we?

In human terms, we would love God to be more easily manipulated and controllable—and custom designed to want the things I want for me—yet time and again, what you get in the Scriptures is a picture of a

God who says, "I am worth obeying; I am worth giving your life to; but realize that as part of the deal, you may not get what you want."

Jesus said, "Yes, I am the one, and yes, you will die in prison."

YOU DECEIVED ME

Jeremiah received a pretty epic call into his prophetic ministry. He wrote:

> The word of the Lord came to me, saying,
>
> "Before I formed you in the womb I knew you,
>> before you were born I set you apart;
>> I appointed you as a prophet to the nations."
>
> "Alas, Sovereign LORD," I said, "I do not know how to speak; I am too young."
>
> But the LORD said to me, "Do not say, 'I am too young.' You must go to everyone I send you to and say whatever I command you. Do not be afraid of them, for I am with you and will rescue you," declares the LORD.
>
> Then the LORD reached out his hand and touched my mouth and said to me, "I have put my words in your mouth. See, today I appoint you over nations and kingdoms to uproot and tear down, to destroy and overthrow, to build and to plant." (Jer. 1:4–10)

Sounds like it is going to be an amazing ministry, right? Yet years later he described how futile his ministry was:

> You deceived me, LORD, and I was deceived;
>> you overpowered me and prevailed.
> I am ridiculed all day long;
>> everyone mocks me.
> Whenever I speak, I cry out
>> proclaiming violence and destruction.
> So the word of the LORD has brought me
>> insult and reproach all day long.
> But if I say, "I will not mention his word
>> or speak anymore in his name,"
> his word is in my heart like a fire,
>> a fire shut up in my bones.
> I am weary of holding it in;
>> indeed, I cannot. (Jer. 20:7–9)

A bit later in that chapter he laments:

> Cursed be the day I was born!
>> May the day my mother bore me not be
>>> blessed!
> Cursed be the man who brought my father the news,
>> who made him very glad, saying,
>> "A child is born to you—a son!"
> May that man be like the towns
>> the LORD overthrew without pity.

May he hear wailing in the morning,
a battle cry at noon.
For he did not kill me in the womb,
with my mother as my grave,
her womb enlarged forever.
Why did I ever come out of the womb
to see trouble and sorrow
and to end my days in shame? (Jer. 20:14–18)

Jeremiah received an amazing calling to be a prophet to the nations. But it was not all it was cracked up to be. He complained, "When I speak it goes badly; and when I don't it's worse." He accused God of setting him up—the word translated "deceived" can also mean "enticed" or "seduced." And about all this stuff about being set apart in the womb to be God's mouthpiece? From Jeremiah's point of view, it had only resulted in mockery, insult, threat, and persecution. This didn't seem like the deal he'd been promised.

Is it possible to follow God and not have everything turn out okay?

THE GOD WHO DISAPPOINTS EVERYBODY

These examples can be multiplied. In all of them a theme emerges: it is possible to follow God and not have your life end with a pretty red bow.

King David desired to build a temple for God. But God told him that he could not, because he had too much blood on his hands.

God gave him permission to arrange the blueprints, gather the materials, and do everything except lay the first stone; only David's son Solomon would do that.

Moses spent forty years in Pharaoh's court, forty years as a shepherd in Midian, and forty years leading the scatterbrained, stiffnecked children of Israel to the Promised Land. They questioned his leadership, revolted against him, and constantly complained about him. Moses got them to the very edge of the Promised Land, and this is what God said to him:

> On that same day the LORD told Moses, "Go up into the Abarim Range to Mount Nebo in Moab, across from Jericho, and view Canaan, the land I am giving the Israelites as their own possession. There on the mountain that you have climbed you will die and be gathered to your people, just as your brother Aaron died on Mount Hor and was gathered to his people. This is because both of you broke faith with me in the presence of the Israelites at the waters of Meribah Kadesh in the Desert of Zin and because you did not uphold my holiness among the Israelites. Therefore, you will see the land only from a distance; you will not enter the land I am giving to the people of Israel. (Deut. 32:48–52)

A couple of screwups, forty years in the wilderness, and God told him he'd die within sight of the land that was promised.

Jesus's mother, Mary, was probably around eleven to thirteen years old when the angel visited her to announce her impending pregnancy. The angel gave her astounding news:

> Do not be afraid, Mary; you have found favor with God. You will conceive and give birth to a son, and you are to call him Jesus. He will be great and will be called the Son of the Most High. The Lord God will give him the throne of his father David, and he will reign over Jacob's descendants forever; his kingdom will never end." (Luke 1:30–33)

We cannot even guess what went through Mary's mind at that moment, but if it were me, I'd have been relishing how great life was going to be from that moment on. Jesus could heal me whenever I was sick; He could turn water into wine and multiply fish and loaves for dinner whenever He liked; He could walk on water and predict the best place to catch fish. (Of course, Mary didn't know any of those things were going to happen; I'm just illustrating how my sinful mind works.)

This is a great deal, if you are thirteen years old. As with Jeremiah, it sounded amazing. Until you start studying the life of Mary.

When she and Joseph presented Jesus at the temple, a man named Simeon approached them. God had promised him that he wouldn't die until he had seen God's Messiah. He took Jesus in his arms and praised God. Luke records what happens after Simeon's prayer:

> The child's father and mother marveled at what was said about him. Then Simeon blessed them and

said to Mary, his mother: "This child is destined to
cause the falling and rising of many in Israel, and
to be a sign that will be spoken against, so that the
thoughts of many hearts will be revealed. *And a
sword will pierce your own soul too.*" (Luke 2:33–35,
emphasis mine)

Notice that the privilege of giving birth to the Messiah was not
without cost. We are unsure what Simeon was referring to, but we can
imagine some of the anguish in Mary's soul as her life went on.

In Mark 3, Jesus's mother and brothers showed up at a house
where He was teaching in order to take Him away, because they
thought He was out of His mind. Soon after, Jesus announced to the
crowd that His "mother and brothers" are those who do God's will.
In a culture that valued the biological family over everything else,
Jesus's words would have stung His family.

In Luke 6, after His first sermon, the crowd in His hometown
synagogue attempted to throw Him off a cliff because they took such
offense at His words. The text says that He walked right through the
crowd and went on His way, but it says nothing about Mary leaving.
We can surmise that she had to go to the well and marketplace the
next day with some who had tried to have her Son killed the day
before. I wonder, if at those times, she remembered Simeon's words.

Mary watched as her other sons mocked and ridiculed Jesus
(John 7:5). Mary watched as her Son, the one who was supposed
to reign forever, was accused, questioned, and plotted against by
religious leaders. And we can only imagine the crushing sorrow in
her heart as she watched her Son publically humiliated, tortured, and

executed on a cross. In those moments, did she remember Simeon's words?

We know how the story ends, of course. Mary was one of the eyewitnesses to Jesus's resurrection and the birth of the church. No doubt Mary rejoiced as Jesus was worshipped by increasing numbers of Jews and Gentiles as the years went by. But there was no way she could have ever imagined the prophetic import of Simeon's words and the journey of faith God would take her on. Was it worth it? Absolutely. Was it easy, without pain or disappointment? Of course not. Following God never is, no matter how much we wish it otherwise.

Is it possible to do everything God says and still have life fall apart?

THE FAITH OF SURRENDER AND THE SURRENDER OF FAITH

Do we see a theme in these stories?

John, you can be Jesus's forerunner and the first to announce His public ministry, but you'll die in prison.

Jeremiah, you'll have a prophetic ministry to the nations, but you'll be the object of ridicule and wish you were never born.

Moses, you'll spend forty years leading Israel in the wilderness, only to die within sight of the Promised Land.

David, you'll be a man after God's own heart but won't be allowed to build the temple for your God because you have blood on your hands.

Mary, you'll have the privilege of giving birth to the Messiah, but you will live a life of heartbreak.

The writer of Hebrews listed many of the faithful men and women who saw God move in mighty ways because of their faith and obedience:

> And what more shall I say? I do not have time to tell about Gideon, Barak, Samson and Jephthah, about David and Samuel and the prophets, who through faith conquered kingdoms, administered justice, and gained what was promised; who shut the mouths of lions, quenched the fury of the flames, and escaped the edge of the sword; whose weakness was turned to strength; and who became powerful in battle and routed foreign armies. Women received back their dead, raised to life again. (Heb. 11:32–35)

But then a less glamorous list is mentioned:

> There were others who were tortured, refusing to be released so that they might gain an even better resurrection. Some faced jeers and flogging, and even chains and imprisonment. They were put to death by stoning; they were sawed in two; they were killed by the sword. They went about in sheepskins and goatskins, destitute, persecuted and mistreated—the world was not worthy of them. They wandered in deserts and mountains, living in caves and in holes in the ground.
> These were all commended for their faith, yet none of them received what had been promised,

since God had planned something better for us
so that only together with us would they be made
perfect. (Heb. 11:35–40)

The life of faith doesn't stop with the first, glorious list. We wish
it did. But the author of Hebrews listed by name those like Abel,
Noah, Abraham, Isaac, Jacob, and Joseph because they are the excep-
tion to the life of faith, not the rule. Those who were listed by name
were listed precisely because their lives were so extraordinary and the
work of God through them so extravagant. But it is the nameless
ones, the ones who experienced a different result from their life of
faith, for whom we must make room. Their lives were less desirable
than the others, yet their lives were no less expressions of lives well
and fully lived in the presence and power of God than those others
named specifically. All were commended for their faith—though the
first group has names that will be known throughout history, while
the others remain nameless. That is not because they lived a life of
lesser faith, but because there are far more of them.[1]

The Bible, unlike many of our worship services, doesn't always
end with a pretty red bow. Time and again the people of God were
asked, "Will you love and follow God even when it hurts?" Will we,
His people, really love Him if we get nothing out of it? (Wasn't that
one of the primary issues in the book of Job?) Or, if you're like me,
are we primarily interested in the benefits of followership rather than
the God we are following?

I want God to simply reward the faithful and punish the disobedient; I want Him to operate according to generally accepted
blessing principles that He gives to us before we say yes to Him. I

want Him to be the big Santa Claus in the sky. But instead we get a wild and untamed God who calls us into a life of risky faith. Erwin McManus puts it well:

> We created a religion using the name of Jesus and convinced ourselves that God's optimal desire for our lives was to insulate us in a spiritual bubble where we risk nothing, sacrifice nothing, lose nothing, and worry about nothing. Yet Jesus' death wasn't to free us from dying, but to free us from the fear of death. Jesus came to liberate us so that we could die up front and then live. Jesus Christ wants to take us places where only dead men and women go.[2]

How many of us fundamentally misunderstand the invitation to trust and follow Jesus? How many of us become angry or disappointed with God because He doesn't come through for us the way we think He should? American Christianity is no longer a call into the unpredictable life of faith but is instead an invitation into the comfort, security, and predictability of religion. We think the cross is the place where Jesus died so we don't have to. And that is true, in a sense. Certainly none of us are called to die for our (or anyone else's) sins. But, according to Jesus, we don't die *for* ourselves but *to* ourselves.

A WATERY GRAVE

The disciples give me a great deal of hope. They weren't particularly bright or faith-filled or quick to learn; they were, in the words of

Luke, "unschooled, ordinary men" (Acts 4:13) who were continually rebuked for missing the point of Jesus's teaching and ministry. At one point in His ministry, however, they got it. Jesus had just asked them who they thought He was. Peter, responding for the group, said that Jesus was the promised Christ, the One the Jews had been waiting for. Jesus affirmed His words and pointed out that Peter didn't come to this conclusion on his own but that this had been revealed to him from heaven. But then Jesus did something quite interesting—He commanded them to tell no one who He was. Why? You'd think it was at that point in His ministry, He'd want people to know.

The reason Jesus commanded silence was that though they had figured out He was the Messiah, they had no idea what His messiahship entailed:

> From that time on Jesus began to explain to his disciples that he must go to Jerusalem and suffer many things at the hands of the elders, the chief priests and the teachers of the law, and that he must be killed and on the third day be raised to life.
>
> Peter took him aside and began to rebuke him. "Never, Lord!" he said. "This shall never happen to you!"
>
> Jesus turned and said to Peter, "Get behind me, Satan! You are a stumbling block to me; you do not have in mind the concerns of God, but merely human concerns."
>
> Then Jesus said to his disciples, "Whoever wants to be my disciple must deny themselves and

take up their cross and follow me. For whoever
wants to save their life will lose it, but whoever loses
their life for me will find it. What good will it be for
someone to gain the whole world, yet forfeit their
soul? Or what can anyone give in exchange for their
soul? (Matt. 16:21–26)

The minute the disciples understood Jesus to be the Messiah, He
revealed to them that He must suffer. But this violated the number-
one rule in the Messiah playbook—messiahs don't suffer and die.
Crucifixion is what happened to *failed* messiahs. In the Jewish con-
ception of God's rescuer, the Messiah was to restore Israel's fortunes
through the defeat of Rome and the Gentile nations. This was so
offensive to Jewish sensibilities that Peter took it upon himself to
rebuke Jesus.

On at least three separate occasions, Jesus told His followers to be
prepared for His suffering at the hands of Gentiles. It was impossible
for them to grasp what He had in mind, so He used the image of
His impending crucifixion as a picture of what was expected of those
who will follow Him. "Taking up [one's] cross" was a renunciation of
one's rights in the first century. Only criminals would take up a cross
in Jewish society. Your friends and family would be dead to you. Your
life as you had known it was over. Jesus calls His followers to carry
their crosses as He carried His. For some of His earliest followers,
that meant a literal martyr's death. For most of us, that death won't
be so literal, but it is true regardless. To follow Jesus is to prepare
yourself to die. Your self, your privileges, your entitlements—all are
surrendered in order to follow Christ. We think the cross is the place

where Jesus died. But it is a place where we die too. The self must die. That doesn't mean you lose your personality or cannot enjoy anything. It means your desires don't rule you anymore. They are submitted to something bigger.

But we are consumers at heart; our lives are built on the foundation of self-indulgence and gratification. "What do I want?" and "What do I need?" are the twin questions that drive us. Jesus summons us to abandon the project of finding life through what Jesus calls the "self"—the way of living characterized by exalting self, glorifying self, promoting self, all in the strength of self—that must be put to death in order to follow Jesus. What has to die is every impulse to assume authority and control over our own lives.

Jesus wants us to surrender our lives to Him and follow Him into the unknown. And if it means a life of suffering, hardship, and disappointment, it will be worth it, because following Him is better than living with everything in the world minus Him. That is what it means to say that He is the treasure. Have we become so refined and civilized that the benefits of our faith have become more precious and more valuable than Jesus Himself?

Faith in Jesus demands surrender. There is no other way around it. The path to the life Jesus offers is cross-shaped. To receive His gift, we must release our grip on everything else. The gift is free, but it costs us everything.

John's gospel records an instructive incident after Jesus had risen from the dead. Three times Jesus asked Peter if Peter loved Him:

> The third time he said to him, "Simon son of John,
> do you love me?"

Peter was hurt because Jesus asked him the third time, "Do you love me?" He said, "Lord, you know all things; you know that I love you."

Jesus said, "Feed my sheep. Very truly I tell you, when you were younger you dressed yourself and went where you wanted; but when you are old you will stretch out your hands, and someone else will dress you and lead you where you do not want to go." Jesus said this to indicate the kind of death by which Peter would glorify God. Then he said to him, "Follow me!"

Peter turned and saw that the disciple whom Jesus loved was following them. (This was the one who had leaned back against Jesus at the supper and had said, "Lord, who is going to betray you?") When Peter saw him, he asked, "Lord, what about him?"

Jesus answered, "If I want him to remain alive until I return, what is that to you? You must follow me." Because of this, the rumor spread among the believers that this disciple would not die. But Jesus did not say that he would not die; he only said, "If I want him to remain alive until I return, what is that to you?" (John 21:17–23)

As Jesus restored Peter, He mentioned how Peter would die. Peter and John had some sort of odd, competitive relationship in John's gospel (notice earlier, John's exacting account of who had arrived at the empty tomb *first*), so Peter noticed John following and asked about him. I love that Jesus answered, in effect, "What's it to you?" Evidently, following Jesus doesn't mean He's calling you to live the same life everyone else will live. How God will lead you can't always be predicted on the basis of how He's led others. I'd prefer John's future to Peter's, but last I checked, I don't get a vote. As much as I want to "name and claim" a life with no risk and no suffering, the Scriptures promise no such thing. A life without risk is a life without faith. And without faith it is impossible to please God (Heb. 11:6). We must understand again that we follow the God who chose the way of the cross. If Jesus refused to avoid the place of crucifixion, we shouldn't be surprised to find ourselves there also.

Many have succumbed to the lie that if we follow Jesus, everything will be okay; and we define *okay* as comfort, security, and safety. Obviously that is not the biblical testimony. What do we do when we follow Him and it doesn't work out the way we planned? Where else are we going to go?

What happens when our biggest fears come true, and we find out the presence of God isn't found in the absence of suffering and disappointment but in the midst of them? No wonder people are disappointed with God when they've been told that God's job is to keep them safe.

Miguel de Unamuno writes:

> Those who believe that they believe in God, but without passion in their hearts, without anguish in mind, without uncertainty, without doubt, without an element of despair even in their consolation, believe in the God idea, not God himself.[3]

SECTION 3

THE FAITH-FILLED LIFE

Chapter 9

WAKING UP

One of the reasons I trust the authenticity of the Bible is the unvarnished portrait it paints of many of its "heroes." All of the men and women greatly used by God are portrayed honestly, with both their successes and failures put on display. Jacob is a good example of this. The man who was renamed "Israel" and gave birth to the great nation that bears his name started out as a swindler and a cheat. With the help of his mother, Jacob tricked his father and stole the blessing and birthright of his older brother, Esau. In the ancient Near East, a birthright was a huge and sacred deal. Esau threatened to kill him, so Jacob fled the area. Genesis 28 records the next part of his journey:

> Jacob left Beersheba and set out for Harran. When he reached a certain place, he stopped for the night because the sun had set. Taking one of the stones there, he put it under his head and lay down to sleep. He had a dream in which he saw a stairway

resting on the earth, with its top reaching to heaven, and the angels of God were ascending and descending on it. There above it stood the LORD, and he said: "I am the LORD, the God of your father Abraham and the God of Isaac. I will give you and your descendants the land on which you are lying. Your descendants will be like the dust of the earth, and you will spread out to the west and to the east, to the north and to the south. All peoples on earth will be blessed through you and your offspring. I am with you and will watch over you wherever you go, and I will bring you back to this land. I will not leave you until I have done what I have promised you." (Gen. 28:10–15)

This text is important in Jacob's story, because it is here that God reaffirmed His covenant promise to Abraham, Jacob's father, Isaac, and now to him. The narrative records a seemingly insignificant detail: "When he reached a certain place ..." The name of the place isn't recorded for us, nor are any interesting or relevant details mentioned. It is just known as a certain place. So why is it included in the narrative?

It is mentioned because the author wanted us to know there was nothing special about the place where Jacob stopped to rest. It is a very Jewish way of communicating this place was not sacred or religious. At that time, the gods dwelled in defined, certain places (temples, mountains, high places, or altars) or were gods of certain locations (cities, villages, or nations). When the text mentions a "certain place," it means that place was not one of these places; there was nothing sacred, religious, or noteworthy about it. It was just an ordinary place along Jacob's journey. And that is what makes God's appearance to him all the more striking. *This* God can meet His people *anywhere*, not just in the temples or sacred spaces devoted to Him. To the Jewish mind, this is central to what it means to be God's people and to understand what God is like. All of the other nations of that time had places where someone could go to meet their god; but Israel's God was everywhere and could be met anywhere, even in ordinary places. Even the common could be sacred with this God.

It is no wonder that Jacob was surprised when he woke up from his dream.

> When Jacob awoke from his sleep, he thought, "Surely the LORD is in this place, and I was not aware of it." He was afraid and said, "How awesome is this place! This is none other than the house of God; this is the gate of heaven." (Gen 28:16–17)

He was not surprised that God met him; he was surprised God met him *there*. Central to walking with God in the journey of faith is the understanding that God can and does meet us in the everyday, the ordinary, and the common. Jacob realized that God had been there the whole time, and he hadn't been aware of it. He was waking up physically from sleep, but he was waking up spiritually as well. He was waking up to the God of his fathers who was there with him in a common, ordinary place. Spiritual growth can be seen as simply waking up to the God who has been there all along.[1]

A BURNING BUSH

Moses experienced something very similar. He was tending sheep for his father-in-law in a place called Midian. It was a place of dirt, rocks, and a bit of scrub brush. Moses would have followed a relatively predictable route in order to feed his flocks. One day an angel of God appeared to him in "flames of fire from within a bush."

> Moses saw that though the bush was on fire it did not burn up. So Moses thought, "I will go over and see this strange sight—why the bush does not burn up."
>
> When the LORD saw that he had gone over to look, God called to him from within the bush, "Moses! Moses!"
>
> And Moses said, "Here I am."
>
> "Do not come any closer," God said. "Take off your sandals, for the place where you are standing is holy ground." Then he said, "I am the God of your father, the God of Abraham, the God of Isaac and the God of Jacob." At this, Moses hid his face, because he was afraid to look at God. (Exod. 3:2–6)

I'd say the odds are pretty good that Moses had passed by that particular bush many times over the past forty years. All of a sudden God spoke and said the ground he was standing on was holy. Moses must have wondered how long it had been holy, since he had been walking through the land for years. Had the ground always been holy and he had missed it?

The God of Israel appeared to Moses through an ordinary, common bush. Let's not miss this. What Moses had thought was mundane and everyday turned out to be the place from which God spoke to and called him. God could have spoken to Moses using any-thing, but He chose a bush for the job. Nothing spectacular. Nothing flashy. I'm sure it was just a *certain place*.

Are there bushes burning around us all the time, but we are too distracted to notice? Am I asleep to the God who is right here right now? As a follower of Jesus, I want to wake up to the God who is fully present all the time.

David's words speak to the universal presence of God:

> Where can I go from your Spirit?
>> Where can I flee from your presence?
> If I go up to the heavens, you are there;
>> if I make my bed in the depths, you are there.
> If I rise on the wings of the dawn,
>> if I settle on the far side of the sea,
> even there your hand will guide me,
>> your right hand will hold me fast.
> If I say, "Surely the darkness will hide me
>> and the light become night around me,"
> even the darkness will not be dark to you;
>> the night will shine like the day,
>> for darkness is as light to you. (Ps. 139:7–12)

Where is God located? Where can I flee from His presence? Is God somewhere else? Or is God right here right now? Is God found only in the sacred places, the properly religious spaces? Or does He inhabit "certain places," too? Is He found in the sacred and secular both? The ordinary and the holy? The altar and the kitchen table?

How deeply this can shift the view some people have of God. Much of our language about God reflects the idea that God is somewhere else. Often in our churches we try to connect people who are here with a God who is somewhere else instead of connecting them to a God who hems them in. We have been in our Creator's presence since the day of our birth; an essential part of our discipleship is learning to live in that reality.[2]

Think of some of the phrases Christians use to describe God's work in the world.

We say, "God showed up" when we are describing an experience that was powerful or thick with God's presence. But is that really true? I know what we mean when we say it—we mean that God's presence could be felt or He seemed present in an unusually powerful way. The passages we have looked at in this chapter, however, portray a God who is *always and already there*, not one who "shows up" every now and then to remind His people of how great He is.

It is more true to say that *we* show up to the God who was there the whole time.

Likewise, when someone is suffering, we'll pray, "God be with them" as if God is somewhere else wondering if He should stop by or not. Or maybe a missionary will talk about "bringing Jesus" to an unreached people group, like Jesus had never been there until they arrived.

Again, I know what we mean when we say these things, but they support a false assumption about who God is and how God works.

Our God meets us anywhere at any time doing anything in any way. Paul says, "In him we live and move and have our being" (Acts 17:28). Nothing bounds Him except His own perfect character. While it has always been easy for people to associate certain places or events or actions with God's presence, God has been busy undermining our work; He reminds us again and again that He can't be boxed in.

Jesus emphasized the same thing. He had a conversation with a Samaritan woman in John 4. Samaritans were offensive to Jewish religious leaders, because they worshipped on their own mountain and not in Jerusalem. The woman asked Jesus where God should be worshipped.

> "Sir," the woman said, "I can see that you are a prophet. Our ancestors worshiped on this mountain, but you Jews claim that the place where we must worship is in Jerusalem."
>
> "Woman," Jesus replied, "believe me, a time is coming when you will worship the Father neither on this mountain nor in Jerusalem. You Samaritans worship what you do not know; we worship what we do know, for salvation is from the Jews. Yet a time is coming and has now come when the true worshipers will worship the Father in the Spirit and in truth, for they are the kind of worshipers the Father seeks. God is spirit, and his worshipers must worship in the Spirit and in truth." (John 4:19–24)

Jesus said, in effect, "Because God is spirit, it doesn't matter where He is worshipped. He can be worshipped at any place and at any time by anybody." This is one of the most subversive ideas Jesus presented. As we have seen, it is human nature to associate worship with certain actions, places, or times, and Jesus—when asked about where proper worship should take place—gave neither a place nor a time nor an action. He answered the way He did because of what God is like. Because God is spirit, He can't be located in just one sacred place.

Jesus does a similar thing with sacred time. Jesus was often accused of breaking Sabbath laws. This was particularly offensive to some Jewish religious leaders because the first thing declared holy in the Hebrew scriptures was time—God rested on the seventh day and declared it to be holy. To the Jews of Jesus's day, the Sabbath was one of the most significant identifiers, marking them off as God's chosen people. Jesus gave several different defenses for His actions, but in John 5:17, He said, "My Father is always at his work to this very day, and I too am working." So Jewish ideas of sacred space and sacred time were undermined by Jesus's insistence that God was spirit and always working. These were not new ideas to Jesus's contemporaries, but Jesus's application of them was. In this, Jesus was perfectly consistent with how God revealed Himself to Jacob, Moses, and David.

STAYING AWAKE

As a follower of Jesus, I want to wake up to the fact that God is all around me and always at work. Many of us live as practical deists—acting like God is somewhere else and maybe, if we sing loud enough or pray long enough, He'll show up. I want to be aware of the God who is right here right now, and because of that, every moment is drenched with divine presence and potential. I no longer have to wait for God to decide to get involved right here.

We don't need more people who are busy doing church things; we need people who are aware of the bushes that are burning around us all the time. It may be the simplest thing in the world, but the most difficult thing at the same time. We need to become the kind of people who are aware enough, awake enough, and slowing down enough to listen to the God who is always speaking. Sitting right around you, right now, are mighty works of God in progress. The sacred and the spiritual turn out to be found in the ordinary and mundane.

Every person, every relationship, every interaction, every time, every place—the Father is always at work. The author of Hebrews reminds us, "Do not forget to show hospitality to strangers, for by so doing some people have shown hospitality to angels without knowing it" (Heb. 13:2). Elisha's servant "woke up" to the presence of angels all around him when he saw they were surrounded by enemies. "Elisha prayed, 'Open [the servant's] eyes, LORD, so that he may see.'" The text then says, "Then the LORD opened the servant's eyes, and he looked and saw the hills full of horses and chariots of fire all around Elisha" (2 Kings 6:17). The ordinary turned out to be full of the extraordinary.

Most of us miss this, though, because we sleepwalk through life. The routines of everyday living lull us into a kind of minimal awareness. Without even knowing it, we consign God's work to our "sacred" places, times, and actions, and miss Him as He moves right around us. We live life on autopilot—eating the same things, driving the same roads, working the same jobs, sitting in the same seats over and over again. And the price for this kind of life? A dull, listless, and boring faith. Our routines give us comfort, yes, but at a steep price. Perhaps that is why the God of the Scriptures terrifies us so much; He most certainly is *not* the God of safety, comfort, and routine (as a routine lover, I find this makes my life with Jesus interesting, to say the least).

God is always up to something, but we often fail to recognize it through the lens of real life. As followers of Jesus, then, we try to cultivate a holy awareness and expectancy of His presence and work in everyday and mundane ways. This expectancy is the opposite of the functional atheism/deism characteristic of most American Christians. For most of us, we act as if the universe is a closed system, containing only ourselves and the situations and problems we are facing. In such a system, we are left to ourselves to figure out how best to manage a tiresome coworker, a nasty roommate, a rebellious child, or a financial crisis. We act as if we are alone in facing them all.

Life becomes the adventure God intended when we remember that God is in the equation—that He is present, active, involved, real, here, now. Because His name is I AM, the basic life-stance of the Christian is *expectancy*. Because God is always near and always at work, we live in eager anticipation of what He could do in our midst. With Him, what looks like defeat is often victory, what looks like weakness is often strength, and what looks like God's absence is often the prelude to His miraculous intervention. The challenge of this isn't in the doing of it as much as it is in the *remembering* to do it. Autopilot is the enemy of this kind of awareness and expectancy.

So we work to cultivate a sense of wonder, awe, and discovery, because our God is always at work in everything around us. We don't magically surrender our lives to Christ because we once pledged to.

Surrender means we seek first God's kingdom by living under God's reign in each of the present moments that make up our actual lives. Simply believing Jesus is Lord of our lives does not magically make Him Lord. His presence must be remembered and then pursued. Charlie Peacock reminds us:

> Despite the overwhelming human opinion and evidence to the contrary, Jesus did not come to start a new religion. He did not come to create a two-hour-on-Sunday parasite culture that pious people can stick on the side of their otherwise busy lives. Jesus came to subvert every aspect of life and culture with the relational Word and will of God—what he announced as *the kingdom*. The kingdom, or God's rule, is what brings a person's life into alignment with reality. To live in the kingdom way is to live a real and everlasting life, beginning the very moment you follow Jesus. This means that everything is overhauled or restructured to fit the kingdom way, the new way to be human. Knowledge, education, romance, marriage, sex, parenting, work, play, money, ambition, business, social services, caring for the earth, even being the church in the world— all of these areas and a thousand more now come under kingdom rule and authority. Following Jesus faithfully means seeing to it that all of these areas in our lives are subverted by the kingdom and rebuilt in the new way.[3]

Chapter 10

POINTING OUT

Confession time. My wife and I had an argument we couldn't resolve. It took us years to work through it. I had twenty-nine years of singleness under my belt before our marriage, and I had, over that time, developed certain habits that were consistent with bachelor life. I kept three piles of clothes on my floor: clean, dirty, and worn once. I knew it was time to do laundry when the three piles were reduced to one. Dirty dishes were left to "soak," and then ultimately thrown away once mold appeared. Bedding was never washed or made (why?). Toilet paper only needed to be close by; there was no need to put it on some fancy holder. I was content with messy.

When I got married, my bachelor-friendly ways of living needed some adjustment. I discovered the toilet paper needed to be placed on the holder so that it goes *over* the top of the roll; that dust ruffles and duvet covers were real things; and that dirty dishes could be reused once they were cleaned. But it took us a while to get me to see messy the same way my wife did. She used to be so hurt because our definitions of *messy* were different. She was convinced that I would come home and notice the mess of our house and just assume she would take care of it. I tried to convince her that my "messy radar" wasn't quite calibrated to her frequency and that dirty dishes were not the first thing I looked for when I walked in a room. I told her I didn't see messy the same way she did.

She remained unconvinced. So I did what I thought was reasonable. I asked for a to-do list.

She wept.

I'm not kidding. She cried and through her tears said, "I want you to be the kind of husband who doesn't need [a to-do list]." I couldn't win! She wanted me to see messy like she did and do something about it like she would.

Learning to love and serve my wife required a new way of seeing. This is true of any relationship. We learn to see things from another's point of view. We begin to make sense of another perspective. The biblical concept of faith is a similarly relational concept. Faith is a new way of seeing.

LEARNING TO SEE

Seeing is much more than learning new information. Learning new information is akin to learning to see in agriculture, business, art, or sports. I have played and coached football. When I watch a game with my wife, she and I see it differently. She sees a bunch of men running around banging away at each other while I see audibles, adjustments, schemes, and strategies. The reverse is true with basketball. For the life of me, I can't figure out what counts as offense in hoops, but my wife watches a game and comments on the various plays the teams run. I have to take her word for it, because I don't see a thing.

We constantly find differences between what experts see and what the uninitiated observe. I look up and simply see wispy puffs of white, but a meteorologist sees stratus, cumulous, or cirrus clouds. I go to the zoo and see cats, monkeys, gorillas, and reptiles, but a zoologist sees each animal in particular and can tell you the difference between an alligator and a crocodile. I see a field, but a farmer sees the crop, notes its variety, and assesses its health.

When we step fully into the Christian story, we receive eyes to see. When we accept and participate in that mercy, our eyes are opened to categories of creation, sin, world, reconciliation, kingdom of God—the categories by which we see reality as it really is. This is anything but natural or automatic. Rather, learning to see reality this way requires induction and immersion into a culture.

The Bible is full of people who misread the signs of God's presence. There are many examples to choose from. Eli missed God's work in Hannah (1 Sam. 1); Naaman didn't recognize God's work to heal him (2 Kings 5); and the Jews didn't recognize God's work in and through the disciples at Pentecost (Acts 2).

John records an instance when a voice from heaven accompanied some of Jesus's words:

> [Jesus said] "Now my soul is troubled, and what shall I say? 'Father, save me from this hour'? No, it was for this very reason I came to this hour. Father, glorify your name!"

Then a voice came from heaven, "I have glorified it, and will glorify it again." The crowd that was
there and heard it said it had thundered; others said
an angel had spoken to him. (John 12:27–29)

Two groups of people heard the same thing. Some heard it as
thunder; others heard God's voice speaking. What separated one
group from the other? Two groups saw a woman dump an expensive
jar of perfume over Jesus's feet. Jesus saw the act as worship, while
the disciples saw waste. What distinguished one view from another?

I want to suggest that in each of these instances, what separated
the two groups is something Paul called "the eyes of your heart" (Eph.
1:18) and what Jesus called ears to hear (Matt. 11:15). Or what the
writers of the New Testament simply called faith. Faith is an inner
disposition or willingness to see. It is a willingness to move beyond
sight (what we see and perceive with our senses) into the "assurance
about what we do not see" (Heb. 11:1). Faith is a way of seeing the
world; it is a way of reading the signs of the presence of God. This is
what so often separates those who see and hear from those who don't.

Jesus talked about the inability of some of the Jewish religious
leaders to see the signs of God's work:

The Pharisees and Sadducees came to Jesus and tested
him by asking him to show them a sign from heaven.

He replied, "When evening comes, you say, 'It
will be fair weather, for the sky is red,' and in the
morning, 'Today it will be stormy, for the sky is
red and overcast.' You know how to interpret the

appearance of the sky, but you cannot interpret the signs of the times. A wicked and adulterous generation looks for a sign, but none will be given it except the sign of Jonah." Jesus then left them and went away. (Matt. 16:1–4)

Jesus talked about how readily the Pharisees and Sadducees could read the signs of the weather, but how they were unable to recognize the presence of God in Jesus. A neglected part of Western discipleship is teaching people to discern the presence and work of the Holy Spirit around them. It is not a coincidence that John called Jesus's miracles "signs." They pointed to something beyond themselves. While the crowds were, at times, content simply to benefit from the miracles of Jesus, Jesus always desired people to understand what His miracles pointed *to*. They were not the point; the presence of God's Messiah was.

Reading signs is something we're all familiar with. We learn to read traffic signs in order to drive; we learn to read the nonverbal cues (signs) of other people that show us what they might be feeling or thinking; we study economic forecasts looking for signs about which way the economy will go. We can learn sign language in order to communicate with those whose hearing is impaired. In this sense, we can teach others how to recognize the signs of God's work.[1]

GOD'S SIGN LANGUAGE

Growing in faith is growing in the ability to learn to read God's signs. How do we do this?

First, we must immerse ourselves in the Gospels. Far too few of us really *know* the Jesus we find in the pages of the Scriptures. Jesus was the greatest sign given by God. He is the "image of the invisible God" (Col. 1:15), the "exact representation of [God's] being" (Heb. 1:3). To see and know Jesus is to see and know God. Jesus Himself said, "Anyone who has seen me has seen the Father" (John 14:9).

For many of us, the reason we don't spend much time in the accounts of Jesus is because we think we already know what they say. We think we've heard the stories, know the miracles, and understand the teachings. The biggest barrier to *actually* knowing something is the belief you already do. I am constantly amazed at how few people actually read the Gospels. And the ironic thing is that we don't read them because we think it's enough that we have read them all before. We may sing hundreds of songs to Jesus; pray in the name of Jesus; have given our lives to Jesus—but unless we continually immerse ourselves in the stories about Him, there is no guarantee it's actually Him we're following.

Organizational psychologists use the term *organizational myopia* to describe what happens when workers in an organization lose sight of the mission or purpose of the organization they're working for. In the absence of clarity regarding the purpose of each worker's role in the organization, the mission of the organization begins to drift and become supplanted by secondary concerns. Procedures, policies, and organizational polities become more important than the purpose for which the organization existed in the first place.

Similarly, many of the religious leaders of Jesus's day suffered from what we might call *religious myopia*. The laws, traditions, and institutions of ancient Israel became more significant than the reasons why those laws, traditions, and institutions existed to begin with. The larger mission and purpose of their faith was lost as they worked to maintain their ethnic and religious distinctiveness. The reason for their distinctiveness was neglected in the process.

The same dynamic is at work today in those of us who spend more time with the religious and institutional trappings of Christianity rather than with Jesus Himself. Knowing God in an intellectual sense is far different from knowing God in an experiential sense. These two ways of knowing are not mutually exclusive, of course, as they can support and reinforce each other. But that is not always true. In the Gospels, Jesus frequently pointed out the religious leaders' inability to discern God's presence in and through Him. This inability nullified their intellectual and traditional knowledge of Him and actually got in their way. I believe the same is true with us. Our intellectual and traditional knowledge of Jesus does not fully equip us to recognize the signs of His presence in the world around us. The Gospels were written to help us recognize Jesus outside the pages of the Bible. The more we soak up His works and words, the more we'll learn to see and hear them in real life.

Second, learning to read the signs of God's work takes practice. If we hear God's voice and listen and obey it, then His voice gets clearer; if we hear His voice and do not respond, then His voice grows softer. That is the meaning of Jesus's answer to His disciples when asked why He taught in parables:

> The disciples came to him and asked, "Why do you speak to the people in parables?"
>
> He replied, "Because the knowledge of the secrets of the kingdom of heaven has been given to

you, but not to them. Whoever has will be given more, and they will have an abundance. Whoever does not have, even what they have will be taken from them. This is why I speak to them in parables:

"Though seeing, they do not see;
    though hearing, they do not hear or
        understand.

In them is fulfilled the prophecy of Isaiah:

"'You will be ever hearing but never
        understanding;
    you will be ever seeing but never perceiving.
For this people's heart has become calloused;
    they hardly hear with their ears,
    and they have closed their eyes.
Otherwise they might see with their eyes,
    hear with their ears,
    understand with their hearts
and turn, and I would heal them.'" (Matt.
        13:10–15)

The point Jesus was making here is that if someone rejected the voice of God and chose to disobey His guidance, then that person's heart would begin to harden and their ears would become dull.

The author of Hebrews warned against this kind of hardening in Hebrews chapter 3:

So, as the Holy Spirit says:

"Today, if you hear his voice,
    do not harden your hearts
as you did in the rebellion,
    during the time of testing in the wilderness,
where your ancestors tested and tried me,
    though for forty years they saw what I did.
That is why I was angry with that generation;
    I said, 'Their hearts are always going astray,
and they have not known my ways.'
    So I declared on oath in my anger,
'They shall never enter my rest.' "

See to it, brothers and sisters, that none of you
has a sinful, unbelieving heart that turns away from
the living God. But encourage one another daily, as
long as it is called "Today," so that none of you may
be hardened by sin's deceitfulness. We have come to
share in Christ, if indeed we hold our original con-
viction firmly to the very end. As has just been said:

"Today, if you hear his voice,
    do not harden your hearts
    as you did in the rebellion." (Heb. 3:7–15)

It is possible to reach the point where someone is so dulled and
hardened to the voice of God that they no longer hear it or recognize

it. The Bible is full of people who should have recognized God's voice and God's work but didn't. The good news is that the reverse is also true. If someone does the next thing they know God is calling them to do—no matter big or small—the voice of the Holy Spirit will grow clearer and louder. So we learn to walk in what we know to be God's voice—to forgive, to love and serve our enemies, to be humble—and this helps us learn how to discern and recognize God's voice elsewhere.

THE REARVIEW MIRROR

Last, learning to see the signs of God's presence and work in the world requires us to look backward and remember. Jesus frequently used images of smallness or hiddenness to describe God's kingdom (a mustard seed, a bit of leaven in a batch of dough, a treasure hidden in a field). The kingdom is not always immediately recognizable and can be mistaken for something else. That's why we must cultivate a way of memorializing and reflecting what God has done in the past. Central to living as God's people in the world is the practice of remembrance. The feasts and festivals of Israel were designed as an opportunity for people to look backward and remember how God moved in the community in the past. They also served a prophetic function, foreshadowing God's work in the future (but that is a different book!).

For example, Passover and the Feast of Unleavened Bread celebrate the deliverance of Israel out of slavery and the promise of God to keep Israel as His chosen people. The Feast of Tabernacles (also called the Feast of Booths or Sukkoth) reminded Israel how God directed His people in the wilderness with a cloud and pillar as they traveled through the desert and lived in temporary dwellings called sukkah. For forty years God faithfully protected and provided for His children, and God called His people to remember His faithfulness to them by asking them to live in tabernacles for seven days once a year. The festival and holiday calendar of Israel was a yearly remembrance of Israel's history.

Jesus commanded His people to remember His sacrifice through the Lord's Supper. We take the cup and bread in remembrance of Him. Interestingly, communion was the reframing of Passover around the sacrifice of Jesus. So Jesus took a picture of God's past faithfulness and applied it to Himself. In other words, God's movement in the past foreshadowed His movement in the future through Jesus.

Beyond the feasts and festivals, God would, at times, command His people to build memorials to Him. A great example of this is found in Joshua 4:

> When the whole nation had finished crossing the Jordan, the LORD said to Joshua, "Choose twelve men from among the people, one from each tribe, and tell them to take up twelve stones from the middle of the Jordan, from right where the priests are standing, and carry them over with you and put them down at the place where you stay tonight."
>
> So Joshua called together the twelve men he had appointed from the Israelites, one from each tribe, and said to them, "Go over before the ark of the LORD your God into the middle of the Jordan. Each of you is to take up a stone on his

shoulder, according to the number of the tribes of the Israelites, to serve as a sign among you. In the future, when your children ask you, 'What do these stones mean?' tell them that the flow of the Jordan was cut off before the ark of the covenant of the LORD. When it crossed the Jordan, the waters of the Jordan were cut off. These stones are to be a memorial to the people of Israel forever." (Josh. 4:1–7)

The point of the memorial was to remind Israel of God's past faithfulness and mighty power. Remembrance was important so that in the future, when Israel was anxious and fearful, the people could remember what God had done in the past and cultivate faith to trust in God's movement among them in their day.

Beyond the celebration of communion (which we may or may not commemorate regularly), most of us have no consistent way to memorialize God's work in the present so that it can be reflected on the future. God's work often only makes sense looking backward, so if we have no way of remembering, we may miss out on His movement in the present. I have been a faithful, if irregular, journaler. I have journals going back to high school. I've got hundreds of pages of dreams, confessions, prayers, celebrations, complaints, failures, and successes. I regularly go back and read them. Every time I do, I very broadly pick up some of the fingerprints of God's hand on my life. Rarely was I able to read the signs of God's work in my life in the moment, but looking back, I can see the faint tracings of His work and faithfulness in my life. By no means have I arrived; but I have discerned some of the patterns that God has used to speak to me and guide me. This allows me to more readily posture myself before Him to recognize His work and presence around me. Looking in my rearview mirror helps me position myself to better read the signs around me.

POINTING OUT

I have been suggesting that faith can be understood as a new way of seeing and that growing in faith is learning to recognize the signs of God's work all around us. This takes intentionality and practice, however, because God's handiwork can be misread. But I contend that it is worth the effort, since God is always at work in our lives. Jesus serves as the perfect model of this, of course. Jesus saw the world not in terms of its ordinariness or brokenness but in terms of His Father's presence and work within it. Jesus would have lived perfectly in the reality of Psalm 19:

> The heavens declare the glory of God;
>> the skies proclaim the work of his hands.
> Day after day they pour forth speech;
>> night after night they reveal knowledge.
> They have no speech, they use no words;
>> no sound is heard from them.
> Yet their voice goes out into all the earth,
>> their words to the ends of the world. (Ps. 19:1–4)

Notice the implications of this for us. The heavens are waiting to be heard by those with ears to hear it. Seraphim declared that the "whole earth is full of his glory" (Isa. 6:3). Paul writes in Romans 1, "For since the creation of the world God's invisible qualities—his eternal power and divine nature—have been clearly seen, being understood from what has been made, so that people are without excuse" (Rom. 1:20). Evidently we can gain knowledge of what God is like by reading the signs of the created order.

But God's interest in His creatures extends far beyond the glory found in the heavens and earth. So do His signs. Paul hints at this in Acts 17:

> From one man [Adam] he [God] made all the nations, that they should inhabit the whole earth; and he marked out their appointed times in history and the boundaries of their lands. God did this so that they would seek him and perhaps reach out for him and find him, though he is not far from any one of us. (Acts 17:26–27)

God has not just wound up the universe and left it alone. Paul spoke of God placing us specifically in time and space in order that we might reach out for Him and find Him, though "he is not far from any one of us." We learn to read the signs of God's presence in the world not only for our own benefit, but also for the sake of pointing Him out to others. Jesus is alive and active in our world, saying that He only does what His Father is doing (John 5:19–20). Followers of Jesus know Him well enough to recognize signs of His presence in the world. Evangelism, then, can be understood as pointing out God's work in the lives of other people.

Leonard Sweet calls this form of evangelism *nudge evangelism.* It is nudging people to pay attention to the presence and work of Christ in their lives and their need to respond to God's initiative in some way. Sweet argues that "evangelism is awakening each other to the God who is already there."[2] Nudging requires us to decipher the workings of God in the lives of people and nudge them in those directions. It's bringing people into contact with Jesus, who is already and always "not far from any one of us." This means we are not bringing Jesus to people but following Jesus into the world and pointing Him out to the people we meet along the way. He is ahead of us, loving the people in our lives with an unfathomable love. He is always working to draw them into relationship with Him, and He is always at work, always speaking, to those who are paying attention.

Sweet uses the image of a radio that is able to pick up the signals that are all around us all the time. These signals are invisible to us unless we have the right equipment to connect to them and channel them into something we can see or hear.[3]

A radio picks up signals that were there the whole time. The work of an evangelist is similar. We are to recognize, decipher, and translate the God signs and signals in a person's life in a way that lovingly opens them up to the reality of the God who relentlessly and lovingly pursues them. God speaks through dreams, whispers, thunder, fire, lightning, clouds, donkeys, bushes, visions, prophets, enemies, and friends. We must never limit the creative means God can use to reach and speak to another.

This means that though our tried-and-true evangelism methods have their place, evangelism is bigger than one form or method. Every encounter we have has divine opportunities for those paying attention. The pressure is no longer on me to initiate and work to close the deal; instead I listen, ask questions, look for connections and patterns, and prayerfully see what God may be up to. I start with the assumption that God loves this person far beyond what I can imagine and that He has been pursuing them their whole lives and is working in the moment I encounter them. I must always remember, however, that what I offer others isn't good advice, a listening ear, or my wisdom and intelligence. What I offer them is the risen Lord Jesus Christ and the good news that He is working to reclaim and restore all that has been broken in the world.

Chapter 11

ON TRUST AND FEAR

As I have written in an earlier chapter, I have had a recurring struggle with anxiety and depression for the past several years. God has used this struggle to teach me about the life of faith and, in particular, life with fear. I have always had a too-vivid imagination. I remember, early in my life, reading a series of books about some of the mysteries of this world—things like UFO's, the Bermuda Triangle, and so on. One subject in particular—the question of the existence of bigfoot—caught my attention. I read whatever I could on the subject. For months afterward, however, I cowered under my covers at night, convinced that bigfoot was not only real but also knew where I lived and was coming for me! Like many kids, I was convinced there was something unpleasant under my bed or just outside my door. But these anxieties weren't passing for me. Whether it was bigfoot, the abominable snowman from the "Rudolph" Christmas special, or any number of unnamed dangers, I was always able to picture bad things happening to me from a variety of directions.

That was bad enough, but I came to realize that so much of our world runs on fear. Entire industries are built on keeping us afraid. Take advertising, for instance. Google the phrase *fear-based advertising* to see what I mean. Medical journals seem dedicated to giving us contradictory advice as to what, exactly, will kill us. Plastic, diet soda, and residential water are just the newest in a long list of potential killers. The hourly news cycle feeds our anxiety, as American culture seems intent on cataloguing all manner of evils from around the globe. The effect of this is to keep us in a heightened state of awareness of potential dangers lurking everywhere.

While it wasn't until many years later that my anxiety became clinical, looking back, I have lived with a profound awareness of all the bad things in the world from a very young age. When I first started my journey with Jesus, I was convinced His role in my life was to keep me safe—to keep bad things from happening to me. He also forgave my sins, of course, and promised me heaven. But if He really loved me and I was obedient to Him, I thought His job was to protect me from all that could go wrong in this world. After all, I reasoned, God said in the Scriptures, "Those who honor me I will honor, but those who despise me will be disdained" (1 Sam. 2:30). I naturally concluded that God honoring *me* included safeguarding my well-being.

The problem was real life didn't work this way. Bad things happened to others I knew who loved God, and after a while, bad things happened to me, too. I was forced to reexamine the so-called "promises" of safety and security that I clung to.

One of the most appealed-to passages for the "Jesus keeps me safe" school of thought comes from Matthew 6:

Therefore I tell you, do not worry about your life, what you will eat or drink; or about your body, what you will wear. Is not life more than food, and the body more than clothes? Look at the birds of the air; they do not sow or reap or store away in barns, and yet your heavenly Father feeds them. Are you not much more valuable than they? Can any one of you by worrying add a single hour to your life?

And why do you worry about clothes? See how the flowers of the field grow. They do not labor or spin. Yet I tell you that not even Solomon in all his splendor was dressed like one of these. If that is how God clothes the grass of the field, which is here today and tomorrow is thrown into the fire, will he not much more clothe you—you of little faith? So do not worry, saying, "What shall we eat?" or "What shall we drink?" or "What shall we wear?" For the pagans run after all these things, and your heavenly Father knows that you need them. But seek first his kingdom and his righteousness, and all these things will be given to you as well. Therefore do not worry about tomorrow, for tomorrow will worry about itself. Each day has enough trouble of its own. (Matt. 6:25–34)

The usual understanding of this passage, at least in the American context, goes like this: God takes care of birds and flowers, so He'll take care of you, too. You are much more valuable than birds and flowers, so if you follow Him, He'll provide for your needs.

The problem, of course, is that there are people all around the world who love Jesus who are naked, hungry, or thirsty. So if we understand Jesus to be saying that if we seek first His kingdom, then God will take care of our needs, we are forced to say that either Jesus was wrong about this, or those people who are naked, thirsty, or hungry don't really seek first Jesus's kingdom. I don't know of many people who would be comfortable with either of these positions.

The obvious other option is that we've misunderstood Jesus on this point, and He makes no such promise here. I think this is indeed the case; that Jesus isn't promising our comfort and security in return for our "seeking" first His kingdom. In fact, He is promising just the opposite, as we'll see.

THE PROBLEM WITH OUR ENGLISH BIBLES

The teaching on worry from Matthew 6 referenced above comes from a larger block of Jesus's teaching traditionally called the Sermon on the Mount. The typical understanding of the sermon is that it contains a series of Jesus's teachings on separate topics: greatness, lust, anger, worry, money, prayer, etc. While this is a common view, Dallas Willard and others have demonstrated the unity of the Sermon on the Mount around a couple of central themes.[1] In other words, the collection of teachings found in Matthew 5—7 doesn't represent an unrelated series of separate teachings drawn together by Matthew for theological purposes; rather it represents a unified whole that is seeking to develop a picture of the kind of rightness of Jesus's kingdom that stands over against the view taught by some of the religious leaders in Jesus's day. It is beyond our purposes to explore this further, except to say this: part of the reason we misunderstand Jesus's teaching on worry is because we disconnect it from the teaching on treasures that comes right before it.

This disconnect is made easier by the way our English Bibles are formatted. For instance, Jesus teaches on "Treasures in Heaven" in Matthew 6:19–24. Then there is a paragraph break, a new heading (in my Bible it reads, in boldface type, "Do Not Worry"), and the beginning of a new paragraph. Surely these additions are helpful. But if we're not careful, the subtle implication of breaking up Jesus's teaching in this way is that He was moving on to a whole new topic when He started talking about worry.

The connection between these two sections (on money and worry) is crucial to understanding exactly what Jesus was teaching about birds and grass and flowers. The paragraph break subtly alters the flow of Jesus's teaching.

Jesus began, in verses 19–24 of chapter 6, to talk of treasures:

> Do not store up for yourselves treasures on earth, where moths and vermin destroy, and where thieves break in and steal. But store up for yourselves treasures in heaven, where moths and vermin do not destroy, and where thieves do not break in and steal. For where your treasure is, there your heart will be also.

The eye is the lamp of the body. If your eyes
are healthy, your whole body will be full of light.
But if your eyes are unhealthy, your whole body will
be full of darkness. If then the light within you is
darkness, how great is that darkness!

No one can serve two masters. Either you
will hate the one and love the other, or you will
be devoted to the one and despise the other. You
cannot serve both God and money.

Treasures, it must be noted, include material wealth but can be
bigger than that. Treasure includes money but also anything that I
value to the point where I orient my life, significance, or identity
around it. My treasures could include my reputation, my health, my
family, my status, or my possessions. Treasures in heaven seem a bit
more difficult to get a handle on. Do treasures in heaven include
larger wings, a bigger mansion, or a fancier crown? I know what
treasures on earth are, but if I'm honest, treasures in heaven don't
sound as appealing.

The key to understanding Jesus here is to understand what He
meant by the phrase *treasures in heaven*. When most of us hear the
word *heaven*, we think of a different place (than here) and a different
time (than now). The word is usually in reference to where we go
when we die. For us, then, heaven refers to "there and then" (somewhere else in the future) instead of "here and now."

Indeed Jesus (and the Jewish people of His day) believed that
God had a glorious future in mind for His people. They just didn't
call that *heaven*.[2] The heavens (it's almost always plural) are the

invisible realm right around us (Gen. 21:17–19; 22:11, 15; 28:12, 16–17; Acts 2:2; 11:5–9; 17:27) where God rules and reigns right now and also in the future. Heaven and earth are the two interlocking domains of God's good world. Heaven is God's space (realm), where God's will is done, while earth is our world, our realm, where other wills are done (see Ps. 115; Matt. 6:9–11). When Jesus taught His disciples to pray that God's will be done on earth as it is in heaven, He wasn't (only) talking about this happening sometime in the future, but here and now, through the obedience of His people.

To the Jewish mind, heaven was less a geographical place to which you could be transported than it was a realm, a reality, a way of living and existing in reality. When a Jew spoke of heaven, he or she meant the place where things are the way God intends them to be. Heaven is not some distant location but a present reality that one can enter into. The heavens are both near *and* far, now *and* then. The Bible, as we have seen, is full of those who got glimpses of what was happening in the heavens right next to them.

Jesus, then, wasn't talking about doing good things so we'll get more or better rewards someday; He was inviting us to treasure the things of the heavens *today*. So much of what Jesus does is show us the upside-down nature of His kingdom. He is calling us to adjust our *treasurings* here and now—to value, prioritize, and reorient our lives around the things that God values and prioritizes; the values and priorities of the heavens. These are outlined earlier in the Sermon on the Mount and elsewhere in Jesus's teaching but are summarized by the simple command at the end of this section to seek first (to treasure) God's kingdom and His kind of rightness.

The contrast Jesus made between treasuring the things of earth and treasuring the things of the heavens is the contrast between what is perishable and temporary and what is imperishable and eternal. The things of the heavens cannot be affected by the vagaries of human existence, so are, therefore, more secure than our treasurings of earthly things.

EITHER/OR IN A WORLD OF BOTH/AND

Jesus began this section by contrasting two ways of treasuring. He moved next to another contrast, this time between healthy eyes and unhealthy eyes. The English translation obscures a bit of the idiom that stands behind this contrast. In the ancient Near East, people who were generous and looked upon others generously were said to have a good eye (what the NIV translates as a "healthy eye"). Those who had an evil eye (what the NIV calls an "unhealthy eye") were those who greedily and enviously coveted what belonged to another.

Because the heart is the true repository of treasure, Jesus indicated that when the eye focuses on something of value, it becomes the conduit that fills the heart with what has been focused upon. If the eye is good, it is the conduit that allows the heart to be filled with the light of what God values. If the eye is bad, it focuses on what it could have but doesn't, and this becomes the conduit by which evil fills the inner person. The previous contrast was between treasuring the things of earth *or* the things of the heavens; now Jesus contrasted between the singleness of the vision of a greedy person or a generous one.

Last, in verse 24, Jesus compared two masters. The word he used for *serve* indicated the work of a slave, not an employee. A person may have more than one employer, but someone in the ancient world could not have more than one master. Another way to translate this verse is that one cannot be "enslaved to both God and money." A slave is the sole property of one master and used exclusively in their service.

I, like so many of us, want earthly treasure on top of heavenly treasure. These sets of contrasts are designed to force us to understand the nature of our followership: we cannot have our own wealth and security as our primary allegiance while at the same time being dedicated fully to Jesus and His kingdom.

BIRDS, GRASS, AND FLOWERS

As I have suggested, the paragraph break and new heading can subtly suggest that Jesus was moving on to a new topic—worry. But I believe that Jesus's teaching on worry is intimately related to the topic of treasuring just covered. He wasn't talking about something new.

Separating Jesus's teaching on worry from His teaching on treasure allows us to force this passage into the common way of interpreting it: God takes care of flowers and grass, so He'll take care of us, too. The problem is this understanding violates the context of the passage as well as our real-world experience of human life. Many who love Jesus go and are going hungry and thirsty today; many are imprisoned falsely and harshly treated; many lack even the basic necessities of life and will die today from disease or starvation. How can we explain this unless we have misunderstood Jesus's teaching?

Remember, Jesus isn't interested in turning us into happy people; He is working to make us kingdom people, people over whom God reigns. God's kingdom agenda is the point—not our comfort or security. This manifesto of His isn't about happiness, convenience, comfort, security. Jesus is looking for people whose primary interest isn't their own self-preservation and gratification. If you're looking to Jesus for assurances of safety, you'll have to look elsewhere.

Jesus wasn't giving tips and self-help advice about how to be healthy, happy, and secure. We think Jesus was trying to alleviate our worry by promising us safety and comfort now in this world. But Jesus knows there are people who trust God with all their heart but go around hungry and naked (Matt. 6:25).

So Jesus can't be pointing to the security of birds, grass, and flowers. In fact, notice His reference to what happens to the grass: "which is here today and tomorrow is thrown into the fire." So His point can't be that bad things don't happen to grass. As for birds, they were used both for food and sacrifice in Jesus's day. I don't think the point is about the security of birds and flowers. The point is the *carefree-ness* of the birds and the flowers. They don't worry about being taken care of. They live fully because they don't fret about their dying. They don't give a thought to being taken care of. Unlike birds and flowers, we have the capacity to worry and set our hearts on the things of this world. We worry, because we make a treasure of things *that can't possibly last.*

This was Jesus's point. *This* is the connection between treasure and worry. Jesus was saying that if you treasure wrongly, you can't help but worry, because your treasure is insecure. What Jesus was doing was so radical that we would rather make Him a self-help guru who gives us some helpful advice about worrying, but what He is really doing is inviting us to abandon all the stuff we store up as treasure, because that stuff and the insecurity about it leads us to worry.

If your treasure is your youth and appearance, you cannot help but worry about getting older. If your treasure is your money, you cannot help but worry about the economy. If your treasure is your family, you cannot help but worry about all the possible, horrible things that could happen to them.

Jesus wasn't saying, "Don't worry; nothing bad will ever happen to you." Instead, Jesus was instructing His followers that if they treasure rightly, seeking first God's kingdom, then they could be as carefree as the birds and the flowers. But if they treasured wrongly, they couldn't help but be fearful, because their treasures were fleeting and sure to fade. Jesus was not pointing to grass and flowers and saying, "Bad things never happen to grass and birds, and you're better than that, so bad things will never happen to you."

Jesus's answer wasn't that bad things won't happen; but instead that if you treasure the kingdom, it won't matter if they do. It's like Jesus is saying:

> What will happen will happen, and your worrying about it won't add a thing to anything; I will have grace for you whenever you need it, and even if the worst thing you can imagine comes to pass, my kingdom is so big, vast, and good, you are still secure. If your security, identity, and worth are wrapped up in what you have, what you own, or who others think you are—all of that is threatened because of the tenuous nature of life on earth. So abandon your fleeting earthly treasurings and grab hold of the only thing that

will last ... my kingdom. My kingdom isn't
threatened by economic downturns, terrorism,
or pandemics. If you get your treasurings right,
you can live as carefree as the birds and flowers in
my Father's good world.

Jesus revealed that our security and provision emerge as by-products of seeking God and living in the way of the kingdom of God. To the extent we seek to secure our own good apart from participating in the kingdom, we guarantee we'll lose it.

WHAT ABOUT ME?

As an American, I would rather believe that Jesus is all for my comfort and security.

Jesus isn't saying, "Follow me and nothing bad happens." He says just the opposite in other places: "In this world you will have trouble"; and "do not be surprised if the world hates you, it hated me first." Jesus invites us to abandon all other treasures. To believe that the worst thing imaginable could happen to you, and you will still be safe in God's hands.

I struggle greatly to believe this. I fret about all that could go wrong with my health, my kids, the economy, the kind of world my kids will inherit, and who will take care of my son with Down syndrome when I die. That's just the start of my list. But what do these worries represent? Misplaced treasures. Because I treasure things that, by definition, are threatened and unstable and insecure in this world, I cannot help but be absorbed by worry. So I spend all my time anxiously trying to arrange for myself the safety and security that I so badly want Jesus to provide.

Jesus does something far better. And far more radical. Should we be concerned and involved with the world? Of course. We are salt and light. And we should be concerned about our families and jobs. But imagine a scenario where you aren't held captive by fear—not because bad things won't happen to you, but rather because even if they do, you treasure the things of the kingdom, which can't be touched. Jesus's solution is so radical: let go of all those things as your treasures and have one treasure—the kingdom of God. I want to spend my whole life keeping pain and disappointment away. And I have been unsuccessful. I have wasted so much time and energy trying to manage God so that nothing bad happens. I am sure God prevents many bad things from happening to me. But here Jesus beckons me away from treasuring things that are corruptible into treasuring something I can't lose.

What we treasure is what we end up worrying about.

So treasure instead the things of the heavens.

And you can be as carefree as birds and flowers.

(Though, I'm ashamed to admit, when I'm out walking in the woods at night, I've been known to still keep an eye out for bigfoot.... Old habits die hard!)

Chapter 12

||||||||||||||||||||||||||||||||||||||||||||||||||||||||||||||||||||||||||||||||||||||||||

JOY, SORROW, AND THE LOST ART OF LAMENT

I have attended (too) many funerals, both in my role as a pastor and as one of the bereaved. From my admittedly limited perspective, I am convinced that the Christian community in America is woefully deficient in what it means to grieve well (and to comfort others who are). We are a "card, casserole, and cliché" culture. And there is certainly nothing wrong with those things. It just seems we should be able to do more for people than a prewritten card, some food after the memorial, and a few token statements about being in a better place.

Statements I have actually overheard at funerals: "God needed someone to make chili" (said at the funeral of a cook); "God needed someone to build mansions in heaven" (said at the funeral of a contractor); "He's now fishing with Jesus" (said at the funeral of my dad, an avid fisherman). You get the point. These aren't mean-spirited things, but can't we do better?

One of the most neglected parts of our worship and discipleship is teaching people how to grieve well. We have lost the art of *lament* in American culture. There are deeply meaningful ways to deal with the grief and disappointment accompanying life on earth that we are disregarding, leaving our people bereft of the resources needed for sustained faith.

Foremost among those resources neglected by the church are the psalms that are labeled lament psalms. Lament psalms are those prayers and songs that complain, protest, grieve, and challenge injustice or evil or God's absence or inaction. They are stark and often hyperbolic expressions of pain and despair. They are pleas for God to act or arguments with Him about why He should. Most of us aren't entirely comfortable with the ruthless honesty displayed by those psalms, but we ignore them at our peril.

THE PSALMS

Walter Brueggemann helpfully categorizes the book of Psalms into three kinds: Psalms of Orientation, Psalms of Disorientation, and Psalms of Reorientation.[1] Brueggemann suggests this isn't a rigid division or definition of categories of Psalms; he admits that some psalms do not seem to fit at all, while others seem to have all three points. The typing he proposes captures the flow of human experience from one of these settings or in the movement from one to another. I've found Brueggemann's work to be helpful in understanding the nature and purpose of lament, so we'll take a moment to understand his arrangement of the Psalms under these headings.

Psalms of Orientation celebrate the good and well-ordered world that God has made. They reflect a confidence in God's faithful character and provision as evidenced through creation. These Psalms call us to gratitude, as they recount God's goodness and support to His people. They reflect a confidence in God's abiding and in His reliable gifts. Life in this setting is stable and untroubled; the world is seen without chaos or disorder.

An example of this type of psalm is Psalm 145:

> I will exalt you, my God the King;
>> I will praise your name for ever and ever.
> Every day I will praise you
>> and extol your name for ever and ever.

> Great is the LORD and most worthy of praise;
>> his greatness no one can fathom.
> One generation commends your works to another;
>> they tell of your mighty acts.
> They speak of the glorious splendor of your
>>> majesty—
>> and I will meditate on your wonderful works.
> They tell of the power of your awesome works—
>> and I will proclaim your great deeds.
> They celebrate your abundant goodness
>> and joyfully sing of your righteousness.

> The LORD is gracious and compassionate,
>> slow to anger and rich in love.

> The LORD is good to all;
>> he has compassion on all he has made.

All your works praise you, LORD;
    your faithful people extol you.
They tell of the glory of your kingdom
    and speak of your might,
so that all people may know of your mighty acts
    and the glorious splendor of your kingdom.
Your kingdom is an everlasting kingdom,
    and your dominion endures through all
        generations.

The LORD is trustworthy in all he promises
    and faithful in all he does.
The LORD upholds all who fall
    and lifts up all who are bowed down.
The eyes of all look to you,
    and you give them their food at the proper
        time.
You open your hand
    and satisfy the desires of every living thing.

The LORD is righteous in all his ways
    and faithful in all he does.
The LORD is near to all who call on him,
    to all who call on him in truth.
He fulfills the desires of those who fear him;
    he hears their cry and saves them.
The LORD watches over all who love him,
    but all the wicked he will destroy.

> My mouth will speak in praise of the LORD.
>   Let every creature praise his holy name
>   for ever and ever.

The psalmist celebrated God's constant provision and enduring faithfulness. He affirmed God's well-ordered world. Each line of the song begins with a different letter of the Hebrew alphabet in sequence—singing praise to God, if you will, from *A* to *Z*. Other Psalms of Orientation celebrate the blessings of obedience to God's Torah or the benefits of wisdom.

Psalms of Disorientation, on the other hand, evoke a different reality. These psalms reveal circumstances of hurt, anguish, anger, resentment, and grief. They reflect a world that has come crashing down around God's people; they are songs of protest, lament, and complaint about God and the world. At times, the psalmists accuse God of silence or absence or abandonment. Or they plea for God to intervene and rescue them from enemies. On other occasions, God speaks to Israel of her infidelity and unfaithfulness. Psalm 88 is an example of a song of lament:

> LORD, you are the God who saves me;
>   day and night I cry out to you.
> May my prayer come before you;
>   turn your ear to my cry.
>
> I am overwhelmed with troubles
>   and my life draws near to death.
> I am counted among those who go down to the pit;

I am like one without strength.
I am set apart with the dead,
    like the slain who lie in the grave,
whom you remember no more,
    who are cut off from your care.

You have put me in the lowest pit,
    in the darkest depths.
Your wrath lies heavily on me;
    you have overwhelmed me with all your waves.
You have taken from me my closest friends
    and have made me repulsive to them.
I am confined and cannot escape;
    my eyes are dim with grief.

I call to you, LORD, every day;
    I spread out my hands to you.
Do you show your wonders to the dead?
    Do their spirits rise up and praise you?
Is your love declared in the grave,
    your faithfulness in Destruction?
Are your wonders known in the place of darkness,
    or your righteous deeds in the land of oblivion?

But I cry to you for help, LORD;
    in the morning my prayer comes before you.
Why, LORD, do you reject me
    and hide your face from me?

> From my youth I have suffered and been close to
> death;
> I have borne your terrors and am in despair.
> Your wrath has swept over me;
> your terrors have destroyed me.
> All day long they surround me like a flood;
> they have completely engulfed me.
> You have taken from me friend and neighbor—
> darkness is my closest friend.

Modern Christians are uncomfortable with a psalm like this. It just ends. There are no answers. No explanations. No clichés. No red bow. God never speaks. The song ends in darkness.

Psalms of Reorientation (or new orientation) celebrate what happens when God meets His people in the midst of the darkness. They mark a sudden turn from despair to hope, from mourning to joy. The surprise in these psalms isn't the absence of hardship or trouble but rather in the sudden invasion of God's presence and/or perspective into the middle of it. Reorientation isn't a move backward to the old orientation, but rather a move forward *through* disorientation into God's healing, deliverance, or rescue. Psalm 30 is a good example:

> I will exalt you, LORD,
> for you lifted me out of the depths
> and did not let my enemies gloat over me.
> LORD my God, I called to you for help,
> and you healed me.

You, LORD, brought me up from the realm of the dead;
    you spared me from going down to the pit.

Sing the praises of the LORD, you his faithful people;
    praise his holy name.
For his anger lasts only a moment,
    but his favor lasts a lifetime;
weeping may stay for the night,
    but rejoicing comes in the morning.

When I felt secure, I said,
    "I will never be shaken."
LORD, when you favored me,
    you made my royal mountain stand firm;
but when you hid your face,
    I was dismayed.

To you, LORD, I called;
    to the Lord I cried for mercy:
"What is gained if I am silenced,
    if I go down to the pit?
Will the dust praise you?
    Will it proclaim your faithfulness?
Hear, LORD, and be merciful to me;
    LORD, be my help."

You turned my wailing into dancing;
    you removed my sackcloth and clothed me with joy,

that my heart may sing your praises and not be silent.

LORD my God, I will praise you forever.

The psalmist didn't proclaim a naively optimistic faith. He had suffered. He had prayed and wrestled with God. But in the middle of the struggle, God responded and acted.

Disorientation does not last forever. Through God's mighty acts, a new orientation unfolds. New life emerges. Of course, disorientation is not forgotten, but somehow there is a transformative experience that overshadows the acute pain of the lament. The movement is then into worship and praise to God for being rescued, delivered, saved, and healed.

TWO MOVEMENTS

For Brueggemann, the life of faith is centered on two decisive moves that are always occurring. The first is a movement out of what he calls a settled orientation and into a season of disorientation. This movement may happen because some circumstance has changed. It may be the onset of an illness, the loss of a job, or the death of a loved one. It could even be something as simple as a growing awareness that life is not always fair and that bad things do happen for no apparent reason. The movement from orientation to disorientation causes feelings of resentment, anguish, and sadness.

The second movement is from this chaotic disorientation into a new orientation. It is a movement characterized by the assurance that God has heard and responded to the cries of the psalmist. God has indeed intervened. From darkness, new life emerges and the response in reply to this new orientation is one of thanksgiving and praise. These two moves are illustrated below.

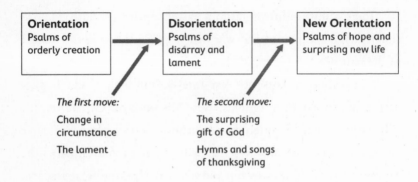

Orientation
Psalms of orderly creation

Disorientation
Psalms of disarray and lament

New Orientation
Psalms of hope and surprising new life

The first move:
Change in circumstance
The lament

The second move:
The surprising gift of God
Hymns and songs of thanksgiving

Brueggemann's categories not only make sense of the Psalms, but human life as well. The Psalms remain compelling to generations of God's people precisely for this reason. They give language to every season in the journey of faith. Some of God's people are able to celebrate and proclaim God's goodness and faithfulness, while others are full of disappointment and pain. The Psalms give expression to the worship of each group. They not only affirm the reality of God's love, but also the reality of life's hardships and difficulties. The Psalms recognize there is more with which to contend. Bad things happen. Circumstances change. Loss occurs. Grief and sorrow break the heart. Life is turned upside down and inside out. But this is never the last word.

This new life (or new song or new orientation) is the great surprise of the Psalms. It comes as a gift when it seemed it might be lost forever. It is important to note here that this new life is not the old life. The times of distress and trouble, voiced raw and honestly, give way to times of newness and renewal. The movement from orientation to disorientation to new orientation is the movement of God toward us; the God who makes all things new, who gives new life, and who brings us out of darkness.

THE NECESSITY OF LAMENT

This background helps us appreciate the nature and importance of lament. There is a false belief in some Christian circles that grief, doubt, or even disappointment with God are expressions of a lack of faith. The idea is that because Christ has come and is coming again, these kinds of raw and unguarded expressions of anger or grief are no longer appropriate for Christians. This couldn't be further from the truth. Lament is not only permitted but also necessary for the journey of faith.

Lament forces us to confront reality. It breaks us of the temptation we have toward denial. It insists that the world must be experienced as it really is, not in some imaginary way. This teaches us about what God is like. All human experience, positive and negative, is to be brought to God. The lament psalms teach us that nothing is out, nor any subject inappropriate. Nothing is to be withheld; every aspect of human life is to be brought to God.

American culture is a culture of denial. We don't know what to do with the reality of death. We hide our elderly and disguise our aging through billions of dollars of makeup and cosmetic procedures. We airbrush even the beautiful among us so that what is artificial has become more beautiful than what is natural. All of this demonstrates a failure to come to grips with the fact that we are all getting older. The dread that accompanies the aging process in America is a sure sign we've lost our way.

Unfortunately, this is rarely different in the church. Most of us don't pray or worship as honestly as the psalmists do. We've taught ourselves to be polite and proper when addressing God, as if He couldn't handle our honesty. Have you ever heard someone pray like this?

> LORD, do not rebuke me in your anger
>   or discipline me in your wrath.
> Have mercy on me, LORD, for I am faint;
>   heal me, LORD, for my bones are in agony.
> My soul is in deep anguish.
>   How long, LORD, how long?
>
> Turn, LORD, and deliver me;
>   save me because of your unfailing love.
> Among the dead no one proclaims your name.
>   Who praises you from the grave?
>
> I am worn out from my groaning.
>
> All night long I flood my bed with weeping
>   and drench my couch with tears.
> My eyes grow weak with sorrow;
>   they fail because of all my foes. (Ps. 6:1–7)

The Scriptures are filled with complaints and accusations, anger and grief, yet most of us sing and pray as if we were ordering off a menu. I don't know of one instance where God struck down someone for being too honest.

Lament gives voice to what our culture would love to suppress and deny. Our typical response to trauma is to keep it locked away from conscious thought. How many families, marriages, or institutions would benefit from someone who simply told the truth and refused to stay silent? Lament is necessary because it names what is wrong and out of order in God's world. The language of protest and grief found in the lament psalms exposes the darkness, names it for what it is, and opens it up to the light.

Hope is found in the midst of darkness and loss, where God is unexpectedly present. The Psalms are deeply subversive of the American culture of denial. And they stand against the polite distance of many Christian prayers and worship songs. No matter how much we try to deny it, our pain will go somewhere. God invites us to bring it to Him. Far from being expressions of a lack of faith, the Psalms of Disorientation are what faith looks like when it is tested. They are expressions of fidelity and commitment. They are addressed *to* God, even if they express grief or anger or disappointment in Him. We remember that the God assumed by and addressed in these psalms is a God who is no stranger to sorrow, a God who is well acquainted with grief. These psalms give words when we are unable to find words ourselves. They are not poems of religious propriety, as if we have to protect YHWH's tender sensibilities. Let us not lose sight of the astonishing fact that Israel did not excise lament from its hymnal, but instead regarded it as faithful worship. Notice that the anger, betrayal, and mourning directed toward God did not lead to the rejection of God. Instead, it led to even more intense appeal to Him.

This is what separates lament from the complaining and grumbling of Israel at times during their long history. The lament psalms, with their language of appeal *to* God, show that lament is properly considered a form of worship. That attitude sets it apart from the complaints directed *at* God that were common to the narratives of the Hebrew scriptures.

IN THE PIT

What Brueggemann calls disorientation can also be called the "dark night of the soul," or simply "real life." None of us are immune to the pain and hurt and loss inherent to human life on earth, no matter how much we wish it otherwise. As I have suggested, God has purposes for these things and will work them for our good. We would rather work from strength to strength, from victory to victory. But life doesn't turn out this way. We hurt. We grieve. We get disappointed.

What should our response be? Should we pretend that things are just fine? Should we maintain the illusion that all is well by continuing with our polite piety and our repeated insistence that God will never give us more than we can handle? Or do we, as our culture suggests, just look for a means of escape? Porn, drugs, and affairs all call to us, promising relief and new life.

But the Psalms testify to a different reality. New life is found at the bottom of the pit, not by avoiding it. Reorientation is found *through* disorientation, not around it. So God invites us to protest, grieve, complain, and plead. God gives us permission to bring our real selves and doubts and struggles to Him in prayer and worship. Lament involves the recognition that answers are usually beyond us; we'll not always know why things happen. Interestingly, Jesus rarely speculated as to the exact nature of God's purposes in permitting darkness and disorientation. Instead He pointed to the sure signs of God's presence in the darkness and our continuing need to reorient our lives around Him. It is remarkable that Jesus wept over Lazarus even as He knew He was going to raise His friend from the dead. If Jesus knew the story would have a happy ending, why weep?

It's because the Bible insists on the truth of three ideas:

1. The utter goodness of God. God is not the author of evil. He never tempts anyone to sin, and there is no bit of darkness in His character. He is light, and in Him there is no shadow.

2. The utter evilness of evil. The Bible never denies the pain and agony of life in a fallen world. We hurt ourselves, and we hurt each other. We have a real spiritual adversary who opposes God's work in the world. The writers of the Scriptures catalogue human failings with relentless honesty. Nowhere are Christians called to pretend that things don't hurt or that evil isn't real.

3. The utter commitment of God toward bringing good from evil. The oft-quoted verse, "And we know that in all things God works for the good of those who love him, who have been called according to his purpose" (Rom. 8:28), doesn't mean that everything *is* good; just that everything will be *used* for good. And the good that God is working toward is specified in the next verse: "to be conformed to the image of his Son …" (Rom. 8:29).[2]

Jesus wept over the pain and sadness that death signified. He knew good would be done to Lazarus, yet lamented the reality of death. Faith and lament are not mutually exclusive.

This requires us to rethink how we grieve and comfort others who grieve. Instead of offering easy answers or trite clichés, we should offer our presence. The Jews had an ancient practice called sitting shivah. The word *shivah* means "seven" and refers to the week-long mourning period when the closest living family members gather in the home of the deceased. They do not bathe, shave, or study Torah. They simply receive visitors, who come bringing food and sharing silence. Visitors enter silently and wait to be spoken to. If the grieving family initiates conversation, they may reply and share stories of the deceased. If the family remains silent, so will they. The visitors simply offer their presence and nothing else.

The day we found out our third child had Down syndrome (three months prior to his birth), we were devastated. We had been holding off having another child *precisely* because we were worried about Down syndrome. We felt like God had assured us that our fears were unfounded. I wish we had been mature enough to celebrate the news, but instead we grieved and worried. Some of our friends were uncomfortable with our being upset about this. I remember one email that rebuked us for not understanding that there are worse things than having a child with a genetic abnormality. I'm pretty sure she's right. But seeing as how she didn't have such a child, her "assurance" rang a bit hollow. Far better was the approach of one of my wife's best friends, who simply announced her presence by saying, "It's not fair" as she enveloped my wife in a hug and wept with her. The Psalms remind us that it's okay to protest, cry, and lament. And that God's presence is found not in the absence of suffering but right in the middle of it. As Paul M. Van Buren writes:

> It is therefore not out of order, if extremely hard to say, that God must have been present in the ovens of the death camps and in the mass graves of Eastern Europe. Where else could He have been than there precisely where His beloved sons and daughters were being tortured and slaughtered? The God of the philosophers may have withdrawn. The God of Golgotha—who is no other than the God of Abraham, Isaac, and Jacob—would have had to be there.[3]

There is room for darkness, lament, and sorrow in the Christian life. So we grieve, but not as those who have no hope (1 Thess. 4:13). Our hope is not referring to something that we possess now in a fully realized form (Rom. 8:24). Our hope is in the complete reversal of death, sin, and grief that was begun by Jesus of Nazareth. We do not offer the world some abstract musings about suffering and justice; we offer God in human flesh, taking the evil of the world upon Himself. We don't start with conceptual and philosophical ideas of God; we start with Jesus of Nazareth, hanging on a tree, humiliated on a Friday, and vindicated in resurrection the next Sunday. We do not hope according to our wishes or thinking; we preach according to what God has, in fact, done in Jesus Christ. The cross is a sign of defiance; the empty tomb a sign of hope. The two signs go together—Easter Sunday could only happen after Good Friday.

The hope of the gospel of Jesus is nothing else than in the depths of human life and experience; among those thought beyond help and rescue, God has made Himself present. In the gutters of human treason and filth, one may find the God who makes things new.

So we must grieve. Darkness and evil are real, and God is not interested in our pretending.

But not as those who have no hope. For God's promised new creation was launched in Jesus's resurrection; the sure sign that God will restore all things … and this hope, as the apostle Paul says, will not disappoint us.

Chapter 13

||||||||||||||||||||||||||||||||||||||||||||||||||||||||||||||||||||||||||||||

RETHINKING STRENGTH AND WEAKNESS

My first encounter with perfection came early in life. Her name was Megan Harrington. We were in first grade together, and she was a shining beacon of goodness in Mrs. Sutter's classroom. I didn't exactly "like" girls back then, but something in me demanded that I ask for her hand in marriage at the age of six.

I wrote her a note that read, "Will you marry me—yes or no?" Two hand-drawn empty boxes sat under each possible answer, awaiting reply. I passed the note to a friend, who gave it to a girl, who gave it to Megan. Slow minutes passed. When I received the crumpled note back, she had only circled the word *or*, deliberately keeping me in suspense. Undeterred, I wrote back, learning from my previous mistake, removing the "or" from "yes or no." Now she had to decide.

More minutes passed. And then I learned a lesson about the fathomless depths of the feminine soul. When I received the note a second time, she had circled both yes and no, leaving me crushed and confused.

Since that time, I've learned a thing or two. For one, I no longer trust six-year-old girls (still don't, even to this day). And I didn't
ask another young lady to marry me until I was sure she would say
yes (which took another twenty-three years … yikes!). But I recall
that episode because it brings to mind the first time I began to be
concerned with other's thoughts about me. All of us can recall the
painful days of our childhood or our teens when we sought to live
up to some ideal—whether it was coolness or being an athlete, musi-
cian, or rebel. I think most of us are pretty in touch with the feelings
of teenage angst at not measuring up to whatever we were aspiring
to be. None of my friends would want to go back to that time of
life, and neither would I. And yet, as I grew into adulthood, I find
the societal pressures remain to conform, though the ideals have
changed.

Now my life is oriented around middle-class comfort, security,
and convenience. The success of my children has become paramount.
Mortgages, 401(k)s, and benefit packages are now a standard part of
life's lexicon. Sitting in meetings or at a desk all day has replaced the
world-changing epic dreams of childhood. I have learned that it is
possible to ruin "Star Wars."

But what has remained constant, from that day in first grade
until now, is the unrelenting, unwavering, unceasing pressure to
measure up. We are bombarded by cultural ideas of perfection in
every arena of life. We are constantly graded, compared, and ranked.
As kids, we must live up to our parents' expectations for us. Then we
learn that our friends rank and evaluate us, and we must learn how to
measure up to them. Adulthood sets in, and we must be "successful,"
whatever that means.

Driving these evaluations and rankings is a set of background assumptions about what is beautiful or good or successful. Every culture sets before itself an ideal—an image or personification of its value system. These evaluations and assumptions are not usually held consciously; they are simply absorbed and internalized from the surrounding world. They set a tone or a framework for what people think, how they feel, and how they act.

Without even knowing it, we all carry around this cultural map, this background set of assumptions and valuations. It constitutes an internalized set of ideas that actually shape how we think about most things, including success, goodness, and beauty.

The real solution here is the conscious formation of alternative, countercultural ways of seeing, thinking, and being present in the world.

But before we get to that, a bit of history.

TURNING THE WORLD GREEK

Alexander the Great was a military genius who set out to conquer the known world. By the time he died in his early thirties, he had conquered everything from India to Greece. Alexander's project, oversimplifying a bit, was to make the world Greek. His desires extended beyond the subjugation of conquered peoples; he wanted to introduce them to the ideals and values that drove Greek civilization. He believed that the Greek way of looking at the world was superior in every way. So Alexander would do more than merely conquer; he would build. He would build temples where the Greek pantheon could be worshipped; gymnasiums where athletes would prepare for contests and sit in classrooms learning the Greek language; and theaters where the Greek myths and stories would be displayed through drama and poetry.

Alexander was driven by the ideals of Greek culture. The process of introducing these ideals to foreign cultures was called Hellenization. Central to Greek thought was the perfection of the human person. The Greeks saw human beings at the center of everything. They emphasized the beauty of the naked human body, the wisdom and rationality of the human mind, and the glory and achievement that could be won through human effort. This is reflected in Greek art, sculpture, drama, and poetry. Human worth was tied to achievement and accomplishment—how intelligent, athletic, or beautiful someone was reflected their worth in the eyes of the greater community.

The value of human life became measured in terms of beauty, intelligence, and military, athletic, or political achievement. What began to happen is that those who did not fit the Greek ideal were pushed to the margins of Greek culture. Circuses went around the empire parading the disabled and the deformed for the entertainment of the masses. Rulers would include the disfigured and handicapped in their courts to show off for the amusement of their guests. This was a natural outcome of the Hellenistic ideal. Whatever was not of sound mind or sound body was disposable.

One of the more common practices of the Greeks and Romans was called the "exposure" of infants. If an infant was unwanted or undesirable, it could be placed outside the village or city gates and left (or exposed) to the elements or animals to die. If a child was deformed or defective in any way, or merely unwanted, the child would be exposed in the wilderness.

This practice is attested to in many places.

In a letter dated from 1 BC, a man called Hilarion writes to his wife about household affairs:

> Know that we are still even now in Alexandria. Do not worry if when all others return I remain in Alexandria. I beg and beseech of you to take care of the little child, and, as soon as we receive wages, I will send them to you. If—good luck to you!—you have a child, if it is a boy, let it live; if it is a girl, throw it out.[1]

Seneca, the great stoic philosopher, wrote:

> We slaughter a fierce ox; we strangle a mad dog; we plunge the knife into sickly cattle lest they taint the herd; children who are born weakly and deformed we drown.[2]

In his "Republic," the Greek philosopher Plato (427–347 BC) recorded a conversation between the pagan philosopher Socrates (469–399 BC) and Glaucon, in which Socrates argued that infants who were born with any disability must be killed:

> … the children of inferior parents, or any child of the others that is born defective, they'll hide in a secret and unknown place, as is appropriate. It is, if indeed the guardian breed is to remain pure.[3]

In his writing "How to Recognize the Newborn that Is Worth Rearing," the famous ancient doctor Soranus of Ephesus, who worked in Rome in the first and second centuries AD and was called, by some, "the most important figure in gynecology in the ancient world," said that after the birth of a child, the midwife should examine various specified body parts of the newborn to see if these parts functioned properly in order to determine if the child was worthwhile to be reared. The child:

> ... should be perfect in all its parts, limbs and senses, and have passages that are not obstructed, including the ears, nose, throat, urethra and anus. Its natural movements be neither slow nor feeble, its limbs bend and stretch, its size and shape should be appropriate, and it should respond to natural stimuli. And by conditions contrary to those mentioned, the infant *not worth rearing* is recognized. (emphasis mine)[4]

Aristotle wrote in *The Politics*: "As to the raising and exposure of children, let there be a law that no deformed child shall live."[5]

In about 450 BC, the earliest known official Roman law code was made. It was called the Twelve Tables. The Roman philosopher Cicero (106–43 BC) wrote that one of the laws of the Twelve Tables required that all extremely deformed children should be killed quickly. "Then after it had been quickly killed, as the Twelve Tables direct that terribly deformed infants shall be killed ..."[6] The Twelve Tables also permitted any Roman father to kill any of his newborn female infants.[7]

The cultural pressure to expose deformed or unwanted infants was immense, but there was also religious pressure to do so. If a healthy infant was a gift from the gods, then one who was disfigured in some way represented the god's displeasure. According to the Greek worldview, one had an obligation to rid the household and the community of the deformed and unwanted baby to ensure that the god's displeasure didn't rest on the parents or their household.

THIS IS MY SON, SETH

My wife and I have three children. As I have written a couple of times, our third child, Seth, was diagnosed with Down syndrome three months before he was born. When we were told the news about Seth, we were also informed of our option to terminate the pregnancy. We then discovered that roughly 92 percent of parents in our situation take that option. Ninety-two percent. As reprehensible as the practice of exposing infants was, is this practice any better?

Earlier this year a study in the *British Medical Journal* offered a glimpse into the future: soon, a noninvasive test will allow expectant mothers to know whether their fetus has Down syndrome.[8]

Current prenatal tests for Down syndrome are invasive and can potentially cause a miscarriage, making them undesirable for many women. But now scientists have learned how to quantify the fetal copies of the twenty-first chromosome, the genetic basis for Down syndrome, with a simple blood test that can be taken in the first trimester. These tests would be safer, faster, and, most likely, cheaper than anything available today.

As mentioned previously, currently, 92 percent of all women worldwide who receive a definitive prenatal diagnosis of Down syndrome choose to terminate their pregnancy. Based on those numbers, what does the future hold for the Down syndrome population once the new prenatal tests are available? Some argue that we can (and should) reduce the number of live DS births simply by testing all pregnant mothers.

All of which leads me to wonder ... Is Hellenism alive and well in twenty-first–century America? The answer, of course, is yes.

The cultural ideals of bodily perfection and accomplishment (intellectual, athletic, or otherwise) still sit at the center of our cultural evaluations of strength, health, beauty, and success.

Seth, as of this writing, is just four years old. He is a wonderful and thriving little boy. But consider the cultural judgments that will be made about him:

Slow.

Abnormal.

Defective.

Retarded.

Disabled.

Handicapped.

Special needs.

I can promise you that if you were to meet our little guy, none of these words would come to mind. A couple desiring to give up their little girl with Down syndrome for adoption changed their mind upon meeting Seth. Another couple that was terrified to have children (for fear of having one with Down syndrome) came over and played with him as a way of confronting their fears.

I can tell you with full and absolute confidence that Seth is a prophetic witness against the powers and principalities that stand behind our world's relentless assault on human value. Human dignity and significance have nothing to do with physical beauty or accomplishment, and yet we see the cultural carnage all around us from believing that they do.

Recently, I read a story about a mother in San Francisco who regularly injected her eight-year-old daughter with Botox so she could compete in beauty pageants. She said she got the idea from other moms who did the same thing to their daughters.[9]

Over ten billion dollars was spent on cosmetic surgery in 2009. Despite record unemployment, plummeting home values, and inflationary pressures, Americans underwent ten million surgical and nonsurgical procedures that year.[10]

A conservative (in my opinion) estimate is that ten million of our young women suffer from an eating disorder. One reason for this (again, my opinion) is the unrelenting pressure on our youth to live up to a standard of beauty that is, ultimately, unreal and impossible to ever meet. Photoshopping is now standard practice among the airbrushed images that blanket our personal and public spaces.

Yes, Hellenism is alive and well in twenty-first–century America.

There is now a fertility bank that advertises itself as connecting prospective parents (with or without good looks) to physically attractive egg and sperm donors. Beautifulpeople.com began as a way for good-looking people to connect with each other to build personal and professional relationships. But the site's founder took things a step further by offering a "fertility-introduction service" with only attractive donors.[11]

From their website:

> BeautifulPeople.com is an exclusively beautiful community, founded for the purpose of creating personal and professional relationships.

BeautifulPeople has been described as an "elite online club, where every member works the door."

BeautifulPeople is the first community of its kind. To become a member, applicants are required to be voted in by existing members of the opposite sex. Members rate new applicants over a 48-hour period based on whether or not they find the applicant "beautiful." Should applicants secure enough positive votes from members, they will be granted membership to the BeautifulPeople community.[12]

Last, two recent studies have shown that applicants who were considered more attractive received more and better job offers than those who were rated to be less attractive. One study found that the attractiveness of interviewees can significantly bias outcome in hiring practices, showing a clear preference for attractive interviewees in terms of higher-paying job packages offered.[13]

MADE IN THE IMAGE

The pressure to live up to perfection is immense. But our quick overview has prepared us for one very important point. Our ideas of disability, normality, and suffering, especially regarding children, are (primarily) socially constructed. The popular images of society that condition our dreams and desires fluctuate and change over time. These forces are particularly evident in our construction of what it means to have a good family and "normal" children.

This should cause us a great deal of concern. I read recently of a movement in North America in the first half of the twentieth century called Eugenics. Eugenics (which literally means "well-born") focused on reducing the population of the disabled by forcing their sterilization, not allowing them to marry, and locking them up in institutions. What does this sad history mean for us now?

Today, desire for perfect children is stimulated through "health information, advertising, prenatal and neonatal monitoring ... and the fear of having an imperfect child in a society that ... constantly measures persons [by] their usefulness."[14] No coercive legislation is necessary these days, because parents "freely" desire these narrowly defined images of perfection.

As we labor under the influence of these socially defined and culturally established ideals of "normal" or "perfect," the church finds itself left with an opportunity to embody the upside-down counterculture defined by Jesus and the earliest Christians. We have, in both theology and practice, vast resources for challenging the Hellenism of American culture.

Take, for instance, God's declaration in Genesis 1:

> Then God said, "Let us make man in our image, after our likeness. And let them have dominion over the fish of the sea and over the birds of the heavens and over the livestock and over all the earth and over every creeping thing that creeps on the earth."
>
> So God created man in his own image,
>   in the image of God he created him;

male and female he created them. (Gen.
1:26–27 ESV)

In an ancient culture where humans made images of the gods, the Bible begins with the incredible assertion that God made images of Himself in the form of human persons. That is, though humans themselves are not divine, humans, according to their very essence, are shaped and formed according to God's image and likeness. Humanity is like God and represents Him, but is separate from Him and finite in all ways. Limitation is built in—we are not gods.

It is humanity *as* humanity, not some element or ability, that constitutes the divine image. The image is distorted, but not lost, because of the fall. The prohibitions in the Bible against murder (Gen. 9:6) and slander (James 3:8–10) are both based on the value ascribed to human persons simply by virtue of their being made in the image of God. No mention is made of their ability (or disability) to function well; no status is demarcated around those who are unfit; human value, worth, and dignity are located simply in human essence, not in human function.

What the church of Jesus has to offer the world is a liberating redefinition of beauty, strength, and weakness. We, now more than at any time in recent memory, may witness to the reality of the risen Christ among His people through the ways in which we value, treat, and love those whom culture deems "defective." But what this requires of us, however, is a rethinking of the cultural values that are far too often embodied by the church instead of challenged by the church.

We must proclaim and embody the liberating truth that image isn't everything. We are to be a prophetic counterculture where weakness is welcomed and people are loved how they are. We must repent of our endless obsession with numbers, rankings, and achievement. Those who rank churches according to growth, popularity, or influence only reinforce the Hellenism implicit in American culture. It is antithetical to the spirit of Jesus to assign importance on people or churches based on their image or success. Jesus measures success in an entirely different way.

We must continually resist the assumption that bigger is better and that weakness must be avoided. As we have seen, Christ's power is most powerful in weakness, so when we deny our weakness, we deny Christ the opportunity to be put on display through us. The church has bought into the American obsession with glory, power, and strength. Instead of announcing the death of the Hellenistic ideal, the church only bolsters its power. Where is weakness on display in the American church? All I see is strength. Power. Glory. Victory. If the church refuses to call the Hellenistic values driving our culture into question, then who will? We must live in a way that captivates the narrow imaginations of American culture. God cares more about the fruit of your spirit than He does the fruit of your ministry. The whole system of church growth and its obsession over numbers must die if we are to have prophetic relevance. Skip the polish. Come out of hiding. In a culture that focuses primarily on image management, we are called to be the community where it's okay to not be perfect.

Conclusion

||||||||||||||||||||||||||||||||||||||||||||||||||||||||||||||||||||||||||||||||||||||||||

KNOWING THE UNKNOWABLE GOD

The philosopher Plato said that all philosophy begins with wonder. For Plato, wonder was that insatiable curiosity that causes people to seek to understand and explain the world around them. While philosophy may begin with wonder, many have observed that wonder ends with knowledge. Once something is explained and understood, the mystery, wonder, and awe are taken out of it.

For those of us pursuing God, we must wrestle to hold both knowledge and wonder together in tension. Our God-given desire to understand and explain God and His ways must be balanced by our awareness that the more we know about God, the more mysterious (and "bigger") He should become. Rather than removing mystery and tension, our knowledge of God should *increase* the amount of wonder and astonishment we feel. As Rudolf Otto observed, "God is a mystery that both overwhelms and yet attracts."[1]

This is the God who dwells in unapproachable light (1 Tim. 6:16) and is called a consuming fire (Heb. 12:29). No one can see

God and live (Exod. 33:20). God is inscrutable, unfathomable, enigmatic, confounding, impenetrable, and mystifying. And yet this God discloses Himself through creation, His Word, and His Son, Jesus. His revelation of Himself testifies to His desire to be known while at the same time it reminds us that He is beyond our understanding (Isa. 40:26, 28; 55:8–11).

And so we live in the paradox of attempting to know someone who is (essentially) beyond our ability to fully know. Our attempts at knowing God are undermined by the God we are trying to know. Steven Boyer and Christopher Hall articulate this tension well:

> Human reason can and should be applied to God—but this is a mystery not based on what we don't know, but on what we do … the mystery of God is based on what has been revealed, not on what has been kept secret. God is *revealed* as a mystery. The God who is beyond knowing fully intends for us to know him … every human faculty may approach God, but must approach God as God—every faculty should expect to be overwhelmed and undone by a supremacy that cannot be mastered.[2]

Boyer and Hall call this kind of mystery a *revelational mystery*. A revelational mystery is a mystery that remains a mystery even after it has been revealed. It is not a mystery based on what is unknown (like trying to figure out who committed a crime, for instance); it is a mystery based instead on what is known. It is something *revealed* as a mystery.[3]

The hardening of Israel is a mystery (Rom. 11:25); the final resurrection of the dead is a mystery (1 Cor. 15:51); the summing up of all things in Christ is a mystery (Eph. 1:9); the inclusion of the Gentiles of the church is a mystery (Eph. 3:4, 6, 9); the union of husband and wife as a picture of Christ and the church is a mystery (Eph. 5:32); "Christ in you, the hope of glory" is a mystery (Col. 1:27). In every one of these passages, mystery is linked decisively with its revelation, its being made known, and yet the mystery does not cease to be mysterious as a result. The mystery is not removed or solved by the revelation but is instead established *as* a mystery.

The aim of our theological study, then, is always to move beyond our study into an encounter with the glorious God Himself; a God that no theology will ever be able to contain. God is *personal*, and persons are never puzzles to be solved, but rather are to be known and loved. The goal is not to get our theology right, but to enter into trusting and faithful relationship with the God whom our theology reveals. *Worship* (and *astonishment*, I would add) is the proper goal of theology. Wonder and knowledge must be kept in tension for the life of faith to flourish and grow.

In America, we believe the goal of theology is to overcome mystery and wonder; however, as we have argued, God is not to be dissected and analyzed but received and embraced.

God desires for us to know Him and has acted in creation and redemptive history to reveal Himself to us. But central to the portrayal of God in the Scriptures is that He is far beyond us. It is only because of His humble self-disclosure that we can know anything about Him.

So we come back, again, to faith. Faith is not naive optimism; nor is it intellectual assent to a systematic body of doctrine. And faith is most certainly not the opposite of reason—an abandonment of our intellectual faculties in blind submission to something that could never be proved true. Faith is not cheerful and unquestioning assurance, rationalism, or blind superstition. Faith, as we have argued, isn't opposed to knowledge but is a form of it. It is a new way of seeing and of trusting.

In the life of faith, we humbly hold knowledge and mystery together in tension. We can know God but can't ever fully figure Him out. And so we walk by faith and not by sight.

As we do this, God gets bigger.

To you, the reader: May Jesus increase in your estimation; and may you decrease. And may we never cease to be amazed and awestruck at what God has done for us in Jesus.

NOTES

INTRODUCTION—THE GOD WHO GETS BIGGER
1. C. S. Lewis, *Prince Caspian* (New York: HarperCollins, 1979), 148.

CHAPTER 1—DUST AND BONES: THE DIFFICULTY OF HUMAN LIFE
1. I heard this in a talk Donald Miller gave several years ago.
2. Obviously, the Genesis narrative also suggests that the man and woman were both to labor in the garden (they were to be fruitful and multiply; fill the earth and subdue it); and the man was certainly to find significance in relationship with the woman (he named himself in relation to her). I am not seeking to stereotype here, merely to draw attention to the way the names of the man and woman relate to their origin and to the subsequent judgments given to them in Genesis 3.
3. This point was made by my Old Testament professor at Talbot, Dr. David Talley.

CHAPTER 2—THE GOD WHO HIDES
1. My friend J. P. Moreland first introduced me to the concept of God's hiddenness. He has spoken about this topic and written about it in *In Search of a Confident Faith*. Several points in this chapter were taken from our initial conversation. He granted me permission to use them.
2. C. S. Lewis, *The Screwtape Letters* (New York: HarperCollins, 2001), 40.

CHAPTER 3—WHY WE DON'T SEE HIM
1. Leonard Sweet, *Nudge: Awakening Each Other to the God Who's Already There* (Colorado Springs, CO: David C Cook, 2010), 77.
2. Annie Dillard, *The Annie Dillard Reader* (New York: HarperCollins, 1994), 38.

3. Craig M. Gay, *The Way of the (Modern) World: Or, Why It's Tempting to Live As If God Doesn't Exist* (Grand Rapids, MI: Eerdmans, 1998), 19.

CHAPTER 4—THE UNPREDICTABLE GOD

1. Rob Bell made several of the following observations at a pastor's conference in 2004 or 2005. They have stuck with me since.

2. Leonard Sweet makes this point beautifully in *Nudge*, 80–81.

CHAPTER 5—THE GOD AT THE END OF OUR ROPE

1. "Made perfect" is the verb *teleo* (which indicates some sort of finishing, completing, ending, or accomplishing), rather than the perfecting or maturing of the verb, *teleioo*; Marva Dawn, *Powers, Weakness, and the Tabernacling of God* (Grand Rapids, MI: Eerdmans, 2001), 38ff.

2. The verb translated "rest" in the NIV is actually *episkenoo*, or "to tabernacle." In the New Testament contexts where the "tabernacling" verbs occur, it is also interesting that all the uses of this related to God are accompanied by forms of *teleo*, not *teleioo*. God tabernacles among human beings at the *teleos* or end of things; Dawn, 47–48.

CHAPTER 6—FAITH DEMANDS MYSTERY

1. M. Scott Peck, *The Different Drum: Community Making and Peace* (New York: Touchstone, 1987), 187–203. I am heavily interpreting and editing Peck here.

CHAPTER 8—FAITH DEMANDS SURRENDER

1. Erwin Raphael McManus, *Unleashed: Release the Untamed Faith Within* (Nashville, TN: Thomas Nelson, 2011), 41.

2. McManus, 48.

3. Quoted in A. J. Gregory, *Silent Savior: Daring to Believe He's Still There* (Grand Rapids, MI: Revel, 2009), 55.

CHAPTER 9—WAKING UP

1. I first encountered this way of looking at spirituality in: Lawrence Kushner, *God Was in This Place & I, I Did Not Know: Finding Self, Spirituality, and Ultimate Meaning* (Woodstock, VT: Jewish Lights Publishing), 26.

2. I am not suggesting that God is everything (pantheism) or that God is *in* everything (panentheism); I want to see God *through* everything, since He is always present everywhere.

3. Charlie Peacock Ashworth, *New Way to Be Human* (Colorado Springs, CO: Waterbrook Press, 2004), xiv.

CHAPTER 10—POINTING OUT

1. Leonard Sweet has a great discussion of God's "sign" language in his book *Nudge*.

2. Leonard Sweet, *Nudge: Awakening Each Other to the God Who's Already There* (Colorado Springs, CO: David C Cook, 2010), 28. This section draws several points from his work.

3. Sweet, 44.

CHAPTER 11—ON TRUST AND FEAR

1. See Dallas Willard's masterpiece, *The Divine Conspiracy*, for more.

2. See N. T. Wright's *Surprised by Hope* and Michael Wittmer's *Heaven Is a Place on Earth* for more.

CHAPTER 12—JOY, SORROW, AND THE LOST ART OF LAMENT

1. Walter Brueggemann, *The Message of the Psalms* (Minneapolis, MN: Augsburg Publishing House, 1984).

2. Adapted from Christopher J. H. Wright, *The God I Don't Understand* (Grand Rapids, MI: Zondervan, 2008).

3. Paul M. Van Buren, *Discerning the Way* (Lanham, MD: University Press of America, 1995), 119.

CHAPTER 13—RETHINKING STRENGTH AND WEAKNESS

1. Naphtali Lewis, *Life in Egypt Under Roman Rule* (Oxford: Oxford University Press, 1985), 54.

2. Seneca, "On Anger," I, 15, 2–3. Quoted in William Barclay, *The Parables of Jesus* (Louisville, KY: Westminster John Knox Press, 1999), 64.

3. Plato, *The Republic*, trans. Cornford FM (Oxford: Oxford University Press, 1955), 159–61.

4. *Soranus' Gynecology*, trans. Owsei Temkin (Baltimore, MD: Johns Hopkins University Press, 1956), 80.

5. Aristotle, "Politics," trans. Benjamin Jowett (Kitchener: Batoche Books, 1999), 178.

6. Marcus Tullius Cicero, "Laws," 3. 8. 19. Quoted in W. Den Boer, *Private Morality in Greece and Rome* (Leiden, Netherlands: Brill Academic Publishing, 1979), 99.

7. Michael J. Gorman, *Abortion and the Early Church: Christian, Jewish & Pagan Attitudes in the Greco-Roman World* (Downer's Grove, IL: IVP, 1982), 25.

8. Zarko Alfirevic, "Prenatal Screening for Down Syndrome," *BMJ* Feb. 2009; 338:b140.

9. Michael Winter, "S.F. pageant mom investigated for injecting 8-year-old with Botox," *USA Today*, May 13, 2011, content.usatoday.com/communities /ondeadline/post/2011/05/sf-pageant-mom-investigated-for-injecting-8-year -old-daughter-with-botox/1#.UbiuS5VoZG4.

10. Jack Cafferty, "$10 Billion Spent on Cosmetic Procedures Despite Recession," *CNN*, March 10, 2010, caffertyfile.blogs.cnn.com/2010/03/10/10-billion -spent-on-cosmetic-procedures-despite-recession/.

11. "BeautifulPeople.com Launches Virtual Sperm Bank," PR Newswire, accessed January 11, 2014, www.prnewswire.com/news-releases/beautifulpeoplecom -launches -virtual-sperm-bank-96783039.html.

12. Beautifulpeople.com, accessed January 11, 2014, www.beautifulpeople.com /en-US.

13. James Poon Teng Fat, "Attractiveness and Outcomes of Job Interviews," *Management Research News*, 1, vol. 23, 11–18, www.emeraldinsight.com /journals.htm?articleid=866683&show=html; "Hiring Practices Influenced By Beauty," *Science Daily*, January 3, 2008, www.sciencedaily.com/releases /2007/12/071206124838.htm.

14. Charles Colson, "War on the Weak," *Christianity Today*, December 4, 2006, www.christianitytoday.com/ct/2006/december/15.72.html.

CONCLUSION—KNOWING THE UNKNOWABLE GOD

1. Rudolf Otto, *The Idea of the Holy*, 2nd ed., trans. John W. Harvey (London: Oxford University Press, 1950), 12–40.

2. Steven D. Boyer and Christopher A. Hall, *The Mystery of God: Theology for Knowing the Unknowable* (Grand Rapids, MI: Baker Academic, 2012), 14.

3. Boyer and Hall, 6.